THE APOCALYPTIC TIMELINE IN THE BOOK OF REVELATION

VOLUME 2: TRUMPETS
2ND EDITION

THE APOCALYPTIC TIMELINE IN THE BOOK OF REVELATION

VOLUME 2: TRUMPETS
2ND EDITION

Andronicus Johnson, Caleb Lee, and Azaria Stephen

http://www.apocalyptictimeline.com

THE APOCALYPTIC TIMELINE
IN THE BOOK OF REVELATION
VOLUME 2: TRUMPETS
2ND EDITION

All Scripture quotations are taken from The Holy Bible, King James Version (KJV) unless otherwise specified.

All Greek Scripture quotations are taken from The Holy Bible, Textus Receptus (TR) unless otherwise specified.

All Hebrew Scripture quotations are taken from The Holy Bible, Masoretic Text (MT) unless otherwise specified.

Trumpet image on the Cover: Credit: © Zachi Evenor, CC BY 3.0, accessed July 31, 2018, https://commons.wikimedia.org/wiki/File:Shofar-16-Zachi-Evenor.jpg, Adapted to be used on the cover.

The book examines how the Trumpets in Revelation match with recent historical incidents, presents detailed proofs, and scrutinizes which era we live in at present time.

www.ApocalypticTimeline.com

Contents

PREFACE

The Lord spoke as follows in Revelation:

> [Rev 1:3] Blessed is he that readeth, and they that hear the words of this prophecy, and keep those things which are written therein: for the time is at hand.

The words above were a fresh challenge to us, because it seemed the Lord was saying that Revelation shouldn't be difficult, but rather be approachable and comprehensible. If it were hard, who could read, hear, and actually keep those things which are written therein? The Scripture above suggested that understanding the book of Revelation should not be impregnable or formidable, and thus we decided to approach the book with simplicity. We thought that if the book of Revelation is easier than most expect it to be, then at least its main message should be clearly discernible.

The first approach to reading with simplicity was to believe that the book was written systematically with obvious order and sequence. Next was to regard the events written therein to be clearly distinguishable into two groups, as either "already happened" or "will be happening in the future."

Such postulate originated from realizing that the name of the star given in the Scripture of the third trumpet is Wormwood (Revelation 8:11) and that the name in Russian translation is Chernobyl. Chernobyl is a familiar term to everyone who knows of the 1986 nuclear disaster. It took us little time to research and understand the Biblical reference to the incident and to accept the interpretation as the third trumpet. Then came the question: if the third trumpet had already been sounded in 1986, what about the seven seals and the two trumpets that come before it?

There are altogether twenty-one events in the book of Revelation—seven seals, seven trumpets, and seven bowls. Should twenty-one events occur in random order, it would be nearly impossible to match them with corresponding historical incidents.

Developing these postulates, we began to research the bygone era. As the incidents corresponding to seals and trumpets before the Chernobyl accident were revealed in history, we also discovered what other trumpet events have already occurred and what have not yet occurred. It also became clear that the rapture, the hope of Christians, was also written in Revelation. At the same time, we discovered that the pivotal Biblical prophecy about the Seven-Year Treaty, which would be confirmed by the coming Antichrist-to-be, was also written plainly in Revelation.

We began uploading our discoveries and interpretations on our YouTube channel starting in 2010. Much of the content of this book is based on the video lectures that were uploaded on YouTube, with additional information added. As far as we know, regarding the interpretations of the seven seals and some trumpets, ours is the first of its kind.

Part of those first-ever disclosed materials were already published in the previous volume. More are included in this second volume, including the discoveries about the sealing of the 144,000 Jews, a great multitude, and the seven trumpets in detail.

After a few months since we started uploading our interpretations on YouTube, we witnessed a trumpet incident unfolding. We still remember the moment we heard the news of Deepwater Horizon oil spill in April 2010. As we watched the unfortunate scene on television, we shared that if this incident ends in five months, then the interpretation of it being the fifth trumpet would probably not be a mere speculation. An indescribable shock came over us when we learned the news of the official finish of this oil spill incident in September of that same year.

Such interpretation of a current incident as a trumpet prophecy being fulfilled was possible for the following reasons. We believe that the probability of an interpretation being correct is inversely proportional to the amount of contradictions found within the interpretation itself as well as in comparison with other Scriptural references. We also believe that the probability also correlates to how faithfully the interpretations regarded the Scripture as literally as possible.

Many still view that the Revelation's twenty-one events of seals, trumpets, and bowls are future events still to come, particularly during the final seven-year period. Obviously, the seals, the trumpets, and the bowls would not have occurred when John was writing the prophecies.

At present time in July 2018, we shall see that all seals had already occurred and so have five of seven trumpets as presented in this volume. Moreover, by showing that the imminent Third World War is part of the sixth trumpet in Revelation, we would like to urge the readers that not much time is left till the Seven-Year Treaty, which will be confirmed after termination of WWIII. After that, only the determined final seven years of mankind await the countdown!

It is out of this burden that we plead that all sincere Christians to delve into this book to reexamine the timeline in Revelation. We pray that this book series will wake up many from slumber and let them see to the day of Lord's return. As for the non-believers, too, we hope this book can reach their hearts and enlighten on how the truth can transform anyone in His glory. May everyone come to receive Jesus as personal Savior and to welcome His second coming!

Andronicus Johnson, Caleb Lee, and Azaria Stephen

CHAPTER 1.
BETWEEN THE SIXTH
AND THE SEVENTH SEALS:
SEALING 144,000 CHILDREN OF ISRAEL

In Volume 1, the seals in the book of Revelation, from the first to the seventh, have been interpreted; their corresponding incidents in history have been identified. The following table lists the interpretations of the seven seals:

Seal	Historical Incident	Year(s)
1st	Papacy	534
2nd	Islamic Terrorism	c. 800
3rd	Feudalism & Serfdom	10th Century
4th	Mongol Invasion	1206–1279
	The Great Famine	1315–1345
	Black Death	1348–1354
5th	European Wars of Religion/ Reformation/Martyrdom	1524–1660
6th	Lisbon Earthquake	1755
	New England's Dark Day	1780
	Leonids Meteor Shower	1833
	Sumatra Mega-Earthquake	1833
7th	Tunguska Explosion	1908

Table 1-1. Summary of the seven seals.

It is important to note how the start and the end years of the fourth seal events have been determined. The Mongol Invasion is dated from 1206, when Genghis Khan initiated his conquest, to 1279, when his grandson Kublai Khan put an end to Song Dynasty.

The dates of the Great Famine incorporate the Great Famine of Europe, which occurred from 1315 to 1317, the Famine of China, which occurred from 1333 to 1337, and the Great Famine of India, which occurred from 1335 and onward, peaking around 1344 to 1345. Consequently, the duration of the Great Famine is determined to have been from 1315 to 1345.

The Black Death peaked in Europe from 1348 to 1350, while in China the plague peaked from 1353 to 1354. Thus, the Black Death is recorded to have occurred from 1348 to 1354.

As summarized in Table 1-1, all seals were interpreted in Volume 1. Reading the book of Revelation, however, reveals that there are two events recorded in Revelation chapter 7 that are not part of the seal sequence. These two events are the "sealing of the 144,000 children of Israel" and the appearance of "a great multitude clothed with white robes."

These two events are recorded between the sixth and the seventh seals which are in Revelation 6:12–17 and Revelation 8:1–5, respectively. These are not seal events, and their interpretations were not included in Volume 1.

In this chapter, the first of the two events recorded in Revelation chapter 7 is examined.

Salvation of the Jews

Let us look into the sealing of the 144,000 children of Israel. In Revelation chapter 7, twelve thousand from each tribe of the children of Israel are sealed. For the sake of convenience, the "children of Israel" is hereafter referred to as the "Jews."

The following is the relevant Scripture:

[Rev 7:1] And after these things I saw four angels standing on the four corners of the earth, holding the four winds of the earth, that the wind should not blow on the earth, nor on the sea, nor on any tree.

[Rev 7:2] And I saw another angel ascending from the east, having the seal of the living God: and he cried with a loud voice to the four angels, to whom it was given to hurt the earth and the sea,

[Rev 7:3] Saying, Hurt not the earth, neither the sea, nor the trees, till we have sealed the servants of our God in their foreheads.

[Rev 7:4] And I heard the number of them which were sealed: and there were sealed an hundred and forty and four thousand of all the tribes of the children of Israel.

[Rev 7:5] Of the tribe of Juda were sealed twelve thousand. Of the tribe of Reuben were sealed twelve thousand. Of the tribe of Gad were sealed twelve thousand.

[Rev 7:6] Of the tribe of Aser were sealed twelve thousand. Of the tribe of Nepthalim were sealed twelve thousand. Of the tribe of Manasses were sealed twelve thousand.

[Rev 7:7] Of the tribe of Simeon were sealed twelve thousand. Of the tribe of Levi were sealed twelve thousand. Of the tribe of Issachar were sealed twelve thousand.

[Rev 7:8] Of the tribe of Zabulon were sealed twelve thousand. Of the tribe of Joseph were sealed twelve thousand. Of the tribe of Benjamin were sealed twelve thousand.

Again, this Scripture shows the sealing of the 144,000 Jews, 12,000 from each tribe. Regarding this Scripture, some believe that the sealing of the Jews with the seal of the living God does not represent their salvation. Yet, the Scripture indicates otherwise, that the sealing is pertinent to salvation.

The following Scripture shows brethren in Christ who have been sealed and given the Holy Spirit.

[2Co 1:21] Now he which stablisheth us with you in Christ, and hath anointed us, is God;
[2Co 1:22] Who hath also sealed us, and given the earnest of the Spirit in our hearts.

The following Scripture also describes believers in the gospel as having been sealed with the Holy Spirit.

[Eph 1:12] That we should be to the praise of his glory, who first trusted in Christ.
[Eph 1:13] In whom ye also trusted, after that ye heard the word of truth, the gospel of your salvation: in whom also after that ye believed, ye were sealed with that holy Spirit of promise,

In these verses, God has clearly sealed His people with the Holy Spirit. As the Scriptures indicate, this sealing is given to those who have been saved, those who have believed in Jesus Christ. This suggests that the sealing of Jews in Revelation chapter 7 is actually an event in which 144,000 Jews come to believe in Jesus Christ.

Research on all seals, from the first to the seventh, in Volume 1 revealed that God's sovereignty was deeply involved in human history. Discovering each historical incident that matched the descriptions in the prophecy eventually led to conviction in the interpretations. This interpretation was possible as the prophecies about the seven seals were assumed to have been fulfilled literally, as they were written. Befittingly, the conviction led to belief that

Revelation chapter seven's description of God's saving 144,000 Jews would also be literal, that God would have fulfilled it to the letter as recorded. Just as all seven seals were fulfilled as written, He could not have mentioned the salvation of the Jews and not fulfill it.

However, the salvation of the Jews is actually a very unusual and unexpected event. Aversion towards Jesus has been the Jewish disposition since the time of Jesus until today. This is evident in the Scripture, as in the following:

> [1Th 2:15] Who [Jews] both killed the Lord Jesus, and their own prophets, and have persecuted us; and they please not God, and are contrary to all men:
> [1Th 2:16] Forbidding us to speak to the Gentiles that they might be saved, to fill up their sins alway: for the wrath is come upon them to the uttermost.

This Scripture states that the Jews killed Jesus, persecuted who preached Jesus, and rejected Jesus who came to them. This unbelief among the Jews continues until the number of Gentile believers is filled, according to the following Scripture:

> [Ro 11:25] For I would not, brethren, that ye should be ignorant of this mystery, lest ye should be wise in your own conceits; that blindness in part is happened to Israel, until the fulness of the Gentiles be come in.
> [Ro 11:26] And so all Israel shall be saved: as it is written, There shall come out of Sion the Deliverer, and shall turn away ungodliness from Jacob:

When the number of Gentile believers is filled, all Israel will be saved. It is important to note that when this happens, the world will be in its last days. This is clearly manifested in the Scripture, as follows:

[Mt 24:14] And this gospel of the kingdom shall be preached in all the world for a witness unto all nations; and then shall the end come.

These Scriptures indicate that Jews will remain "blind" to the truth and remain unbelieving until the last days, when the gospel will have reached all nations in the world. Thus, until the end times, a Jew's profession of faith in Jesus as personal Messiah will be a very rare occurrence.

How then, will the Jews come to salvation in the last days? According to the Scripture, the salvation of the Jews will be during the last war before the millennial kingdom, when the Lord will return to lead the battle to victory. At that time, the Jews will collectively repent and come to believe in Lord Jesus. This topic will be thoroughly discussed in Volume 4.

Again, a Jew's conversion to Christianity is expected to be a very rare incident until the last days. Consequently, people will have difficult time believing that a large number of Jews would accept Jesus as their personal Savior. Instead, people will most likely be skeptical and unbelieving about the conversion of many Jews into Christianity.

In Revelation chapter 7, however, the sealing of Jews is done; the unlikely conversion of Jews into Christianity occurs. It is certainly not a collective salvation of all Jews, but the sealing is provided to 144,000 Jews, who believe in Jesus Christ as their personal Savior. Contrary to popular notion that this event in Revelation chapter 7 occurs during Daniel's seventieth week, the final seven years of mankind, this happens between the sixth seal and the first trumpet, as will be discussed hereafter. This indicates that this salvation of the 144,000 Jews, an unusual and unexpected incident, had already taken place in history. In this chapter, the evidences of this historical incident are presented.

Before moving on with further interpretation of this event, it is worthwhile to mention that many rely on the numerology of

144,000 in interpreting this event, rather than on literal interpretation. This popular approach is perhaps highly influenced by the extreme unlikelihood of Jews' believing in Jesus before the last days and the persistent persecution of Jews throughout history. Yet, this approach may be subject to prejudice and/or failure to believe in God's sovereignty in the prophesied events being fulfilled in history, regardless of the difficulty or unlikelihood. Certainly, meanings in the numbers in the Bible cannot entirely be neglected. However, if God cannot fulfill in history what He declared in the Bible, then where would be the foundation of Christian faith in God?

Timing of the Salvation of 144,000 Jews

In the book of Revelation, the sealing of the 144,000 Jews in chapter 7 is recorded between the sixth and the seventh seals which are in Revelation 6:12–17 and Revelation 8:1–5, respectively. Based on this order, one might naturally speculate that the sealing event must have been fulfilled after 1833 when the sixth seal had been fulfilled and before 1908 when the seventh seal had been opened. However, scrutinizing the Scripture reveals that this is not the case.

To understand why, it is important to note that this sealing event is not part of the sixth seal. In fact, the two events described in Revelation chapter 7 are not seal events, and thus, are not part of the seal sequence. This means that although these events occur between the sixth and seventh seals, they do not necessarily have to finish before the opening of the seventh seal. As will be discussed later, the second event in Revelation chapter 7, "a great multitude clothed with white robes," continues even after the opening of the seventh seal.

The first event in Revelation chapter 7, the "sealing of the 144,000 Jews," begins between the sixth and seventh seals and comes to an end before the sounding of the first trumpet, not before the seventh seal. According to Revelation 7:1 and 7:3, the sealing event occurs while four angels are holding the four winds of the earth in order that no wind blows on the earth, the sea, or any tree. The Scripture reads as follows:

> [Rev 7:1] And after these things I saw four angels standing on the four corners of the earth, holding the four winds of the earth, that the wind should not blow on the earth, nor on the sea, nor on any tree.
> [Rev 7:3] Saying, Hurt not the earth, neither the sea, nor the trees, till we have sealed the servants of our God in their foreheads.

This windless condition, which prevents the earth, the sea, and the trees from being hurt, comes to an end with the completion of sealing of the 144,000 Jews. In Revelation 8:7, the first trumpet is sounded and the earth and the trees are hurt. In Revelation 8:8, the second trumpet is sounded and the sea is hurt. These can be seen in the following Scripture:

> [Rev 8:7] The first angel sounded, and there followed hail and fire mingled with blood, and they were cast upon the earth: and the third part of trees was burnt up, and all green grass was burnt up.
> [Rev 8:8] And the second angel sounded, and as it were a great mountain burning with fire was cast into the sea: and the third part of the sea became blood;

In the Scripture above, the earth, the sea, and the trees are hurt, indicating that the windless condition has ended. As will be discussed in later chapters, the first trumpet in verse 7 corresponds to the First World War, during which the earth and the trees are hurt. The second trumpet in verse 8 corresponds to the Second World War, during which the sea is hurt.

The fact that the first and the second trumpets are the first two world wars agrees with the phenomena of "the earth, the sea, and the trees" being hurt by the "four winds" blowing on the earth, the sea, and the trees. Revelation chapter 7 shows that while the "four winds" are held by four angels, the earth, the sea, and the trees are not hurt. As will be elaborated in Volume 4, the "four winds" in this context signify a big war, as is suggested in the following Scripture from the Old Testament:

> [Jer 49:36] And upon Elam will I bring the four winds from the four quarters of heaven, and will scatter them toward all those winds; and there shall be no nation whither the outcasts of Elam shall not come.

The Scripture above describes the "four winds" as causing scattering of a nation's population through military forces. In World War I and World War II, both global-scale wars, the "four winds" are no longer held by the "four angels" in Revelation 7:1. Consequently, earth, sea, and trees are hurt.

Then what about during the seventh seal? Are the "four winds" released and blowing? The Scripture reveals that the "four winds" are still held by the four angels during the seventh seal. The seventh seal, the Tunguska blast, is described in Revelation 8:1–5 and involves an earthquake among various phenomena. As elaborated in Volume 1, during the seventh seal, a golden censer filled with fire is cast into the earth, causing trees to burn and fall flat to the ground and creating seismic waves. Clearly, the seventh seal involves some kind of an effect on the earth and the trees. However, the fact that there is no warfare involved suggests that the "four winds" that hurt the earth, the sea, and the trees through military forces are still being held by the four angels.

The "four angels" in Revelation 7:1 are not allowed to hurt the earth, the sea, and the trees with the "four winds" until the sealing of the 144,000 Jews is completed, as indicated in Revelation 7:2–3.

The fact the "four winds" are finally released and involved in the first and second trumpets explains that the sealing of the 144,000 Jews continues throughout the seventh seal and is completed before the sounding of the first trumpet.

The fact that this event is recorded between the sixth and the seventh seals, yet is not part of the sixth seal, deserves special attention. What makes it unique is that the event does not end before the seventh seal but continues on until the first trumpet blows. As evident from what God revealed in the Scripture, the four winds of the earth are held tight. In other words, the First World War is prevented from happening, until the sealing comes to completion.

If this event of sealing 144,000 Jews were a part of the sixth seal, the event should have completed before the seventh seal was opened, because all the seals happen in sequential order. The next seal in the sequence cannot be opened prior to the completion of the previous seal, or at least until after the incident of the previous seal has climaxed. This clearly indicates that the "sealing 144,000 children of Israel" event does not belong to the seal series, as it violates the principle that the seals are opened one after another in a sequential manner. As the sealing is not a part of the sixth seal, no time restriction applies; the sealing does not have to be completed before the opening of the seventh seal. Instead, God has put a different restriction: the sealing must be completed before World War I.

The seventh seal is the Tunguska explosion of 1908, whereas the first trumpet is World War I that started in 1914. To be accurate, the sealing of the Jews would have started after the completion of the sixth seal in 1833 and continued until the year 1914 at the latest. This duration is different from that of the second event in Revelation 7, in which the Apostle John witnesses a great multitude. Details of the second event will be examined in the next chapter.

In summary, the Scripture indicates that 144,000 Jews are saved during a period with no big wars, between the completion of the sixth seal and the start of World War I.

Absence of Big Wars from 1833 to 1914

As the "four winds" were being held in order to prevent big wars, there would have been no wars while the 144,000 Jews were being sealed. Therefore, the first step in interpreting this "sealing" event was examining for absence of big wars around the period of 1833 to 1914.

First, Europe was examined. As a result of the Industrial Revolution that began in 1760s, Europe had transformed into a developed region with its advanced industry and revolutionary technology. Historian Kenneth Scott Latourette testifies that: "The nineteenth century, beginning in 1815 with the close of the Wars of the French Revolution and Napoleon and terminated in 1914 by the outbreak of World War I, saw the heyday [flourishing time] of Western imperialism and colonialism."[1]

He further notes that other than the American Civil War (1861–1865) and China's Taiping Rebellion (1850–1865) there was no significant war during the century:

> Now and again wars were fought in Europe—the chief being the Crimean War (1854–1856) and the Franco-Prussian War (1870–1871)—but they did not draw all Europe into their vortex, as several earlier ones had done, and they were relatively brief. Here and there conflicts arose from imperial expansion, as in the Boer War (1899–1902) and the Russo-Japanese War (1904–1905). But only these two seriously challenged a European power. They were late in the century and in retrospect were seen to be the twilight of an era. By the

year 1914 European peoples had made themselves the
rulers of most of the planet.[2]

According to the historical records, the majority of the
nineteenth century and the early twentieth century were indeed a
period during which God "held the four winds of the earth,"
preventing a worldwide war from happening. Confirmation of
this detail led to the next question: what relation did this absence
of big wars have with the Jews? As anti-Semitism had persisted
throughout history and even led to mass persecutions and
murders as in the Holocaust, research was done to examine the
history of Jewish persecution.

As commonly known, Jews have been the target of much
persecution throughout history. According to *History of Hatred
against Jews* at glennbeck.com, from 175 to 163 BC, there were
attempts to outlaw Judaism. In AD 72, Jews were expelled from
Palestine. From the fifteenth century to 1772, they were banned in
Russia. In 1925, the book *Mein Kampf* by Adolf Hitler was
published. Careful examination of history revealed that after
persecution of Jews in 1555, 1648 to 1649, and 1772, there was no
notable persecution until Hitler came to power.[3]

This notable absence of persecution was during the nineteenth
century. During this time, persecution of Jews died down for quite
a long time, in contrast to continued persecution that had existed
throughout history. This period coincided with the period that
had no big wars and suggested that this was also the period
described in Revelation chapter 7.

In fact, there were persecutions of Jews in the nineteenth
century also. Pogroms in the late nineteenth and the early
twentieth centuries in the Russian Empire are examples. In
general, however, in the nineteenth century, there was not much
persecution of Jews.

In further interpretation of the "sealing of the 144,000 Jews"
event, it was important to examine whether there was conversion

of Jews during the period that had no big wars and persecution of Jews. Research revealed that, prior to the nineteenth century, there have been rather unsuccessful efforts among the Roman Catholic and Protestant churches to convert the Jews. However, during the nineteenth century, many Jews converted as a result of successful missions taken by the churches. The next sections discuss these efforts.

Mission to the Jews in the Roman Catholic Church

In His first coming, the Lord preached to the Jewish people. Not to mention, His twelve disciples were also Jews. What is more, a great number of believers in the early church were of the priesthood, and altogether there were tens of thousands of Jewish believers (Ac 6:7; 21:20).

After the Ascension of Jesus, many Jews continued to become Christians, in which the Roman Catholic Church played a part. Although driven by political motives, Justinian I (c. 482–565), the emperor of the Eastern Roman (or Byzantine) Empire, decreed to use Greek and Latin translation of the Old Testament in the Jewish synagogues and to disallow Talmudic exegesis in order to lead the Jews to Christianity.

Such efforts to proselytize Jews continued within the Roman Catholic Church as well. Pope Gregory I (c. 540–604) condemned the practice of compulsory baptism and rather tried to win Jews for the church through kindness and compensational methods.[4] Such extraordinary attempts during the time can be summarized in the following excerpt:

> There was hardly a century that works were not written to bring about the conversion of the Jews, hardly one in which rewards were not offered to secure them for the Church, and also not a century in which numbers of proselytes, thoroughly convinced,

25

did not pass over to Christianity, many of whom became an honor to the Church.[5]

Similar efforts by Roman Catholics to convert Jews were especially conspicuous in Spain region. In 686, Bishop Julian of Toledo (642–690) wrote *De Comprobatione Aetatis Sextae Contra Judaeos* (*About the Evidence of the Sixth Period Against Jews*), the sole purpose of which was to disprove Jews' erroneous preconception that Jesus cannot be the Messiah. Raymond of Pennaforte (c. 1175–1275), a Dominican friar, began teaching the Hebrew language and Talmudic writings in his order to promote mission works targeting Jews.[6,7]

Pablo Christiani of Montpellier of the thirteenth century was a Jew and later proselytized to Christianity and became a Dominican friar. In a sense, he was the first real Christian missionary preacher who was of Jewish origin. He traveled through southern France and other regions to preach in churches and synagogues, disputed with Jews, proclaimed the divinity of Christ from the Bible and Talmud, and professed Jesus as the Messiah.[8]

Benedict XIII (1328–1423), an antipope, was also interested in converting Jews in his whole life. At the early fifteenth century, the Dominican Vincent Ferrer (1350–1419) evangelized in Italy, France, and Spain, and in Castile and Aragon, and at least 20,500 were baptized.[9]

In France, there was a comparatively meager effort by the Catholic Church. However, in Italy, both power and monks were very much interested in converting Jews. Pope Paul III (1468–1549) of Rome even established an institution for that expressed purpose, and Pius V (1504–1572) succeeded in proselytizing over one hundred of intellectual and affluent Jews.[10]

The situation in England was somewhat unique. During the reign of King William Rufus (c. 1056–1100), Jews complained of too many Jews converting to Christianity. During the reign of

King Edward I (1239–1307), five hundred Jewish proselytes received baptism. However, by 1290, almost all Jews were expelled from England and until the year 1655 hardly any official record of Jewish presence was found in England.[11]

Germany differed from England the most in that there is "no record of any missionary efforts, but only of compulsory baptisms occasioned by the persecutions during the crusades, the invasions of the Tatars, and the Black Death."[12]

Modern efforts of Roman Catholics to convert Jews began in France. The furthest-reaching efforts are visible from the proselyte Maria Alphonse Ratisbonne (1814–1884), who founded Congrégation de Notre-Dame de Sion (Congregation of Our Lady of Sion) in Palestine for educating Jewish girls and organized numerous charitable institutions in France, England, Chalcedon, Galatia, and elsewhere including Palestine.[13]

Mission to the Jews in Protestant Churches

Protestant Churches also played a big role in converting Jews, a very difficult mission. Martin Luther (1483–1546), who was initially well disposed to converting Jews, reverted to a stance that all efforts are futile. The following quote by Luther unveils how difficult and pessimistic proselytizing efforts are: "It is as easy to convert Jews as to convert the devil himself."[14]

Nevertheless, there were numerous Jewish converts in Lutheran and Reformed churches. The first organizational efforts to reach out to Jews appeared at the synods of Dordrecht, Delft, and Leyden in Holland between 1676 and 1678.[15]

Ezra Edzard (1629–1708) of Hamburg was especially zealous for the cause and continued in the ministry with his sons, Georg and Sebastian, through self-financing. Similar funds supported evangelizing the Jews in many places such as Geneva, Darmstadt, and Frankfort.[16]

However, these efforts mostly proved ineffectual. The official record from Darmstadt wrote: "In 1736, '400 erring sheep were admitted into the Christian fold, and 600 impostors were refused admission.'"[17]

Moravian Samuel Lieberkühn (1710–1777) labored for 30 years among the Jews, and Callenberg founded Institutum Judaicum (Jewish Institute) in 1728, which continued operation till 1792. Two missionaries from the institution went around provinces in Poland, Bohemia, Germany, Denmark, and England from 1730 to 1735. In 1736, Stephan Schulz joined the mission and extended the region to all Europe and as far as the Orient.[18] Nonetheless, their efforts also remained unprofitable.[19] However, one of the tangible rewards that resulted from churches' tireless efforts was gradual renunciation of the Talmud by groups of liberal Jews.

Moreover, secularly, vivid societal changes followed in that Jews, further instigated by churches vilifying those who still held to Jewish roots, converted to Christianity for political and socioeconomic reasons:

> The upper classes of Jews in Germany, Austria, and France gradually broke away from their ancestral religion, which appeared to them as a shackle and a misfortune, and felt no scruple in taking a step which was the only means of freeing the Jew in the eyes of the Christian world from the yoke and the shame of centuries. Not from conviction, but attracted by the hope of brilliant careers or grand alliances, hundreds of Jewish families in Berlin, Vienna, Königsberg, and elsewhere joined the Church, "fluttering like moths around the flame until they were consumed." . . . In fact, government and Church, press and people, conspired to render the life of the Jew as miserable as possible, a continual martyrdom, while the strong conviction which produced martyrs in former ages

was lacking. And as if to deprive the Jew of every spark of self-respecting manhood, it was made part of the Pharaonic system to declare the Jewish persuasion to be a disqualification for governmental offices and posts of honor in civic life or in the army, and at the same time to bribe Jewish men of letters and learning by offering them promotion in case they would change their faith.[20]

Therefore, there were overflowing numbers of Jews converting to Christianity, yet purely out of worldly motives.

Mission to the Jews in the 19th century

Although many efforts before the nineteenth century were of little avail in proselytizing the Jews, the Protestant churches began to reap what they sowed beginning from the nineteenth century. In Germany, especially from Berlin, many Jews became Christians, and about 3,984 upscale and cultured Jews received baptism from 1816 to 1843.[21]

Meanwhile in England, the Jews expelled out of the country in 1290 slowly began to return and resettle starting in 1655. Toward the end of the seventeenth century, there were a large number of Jewish immigrants from Germany and Poland. By 1753, the Jewish Naturalization Act had passed, granting Jews with all the rights of British subjects. But due to fierce opposition, the Act was repealed in 1754. Therefore, there were still many restrictions for Jews, such as the mandated Christian oath of office that deprived Jews' eligibility for the Parliament.[22]

Consequently, Jews in England were continually pressured to convert to Christianity. Although "a bill for the total removal of Jewish disabilities" passed the House of Commons in 1833, 1834, and 1836, it was turned down by the House of Lords each time.

Eventually, a bill was passed in 1858, emancipating Jews from eligibility restrictions.[23]

On another note, the churches and their institutions in England became so corrupt that many Christians believed the end time was near and expected to see many Jews turn to the Lord.[24]

By 1809, the London Society for the Promotion of Christianity among the Jews (the London Society) was established in England, inspired by genuine love for the Jewish people. Among its patrons were "several highly influential figures in British governmental and clerical circles." [25] Although it initially targeted the impoverished Jews in London, later it strived to convert Jews of all social classes. Such endeavor, however, faced criticism from many that "the time, money, and energy being expended to convert a Jew might more profitably be devoted to bringing some of Protestantism's own lost sheep back into the fold."[26]

In spite of criticism, the members of the London Society believed that their continual outreach to Jews would pay off at God's ripe time in massive converts to Anglican Christianity.[27] The efforts led to a considerable number of baptized Jews, but the plan in 1832 to build a Hebrew-Christian Church in England failed. As such, the London Society was "the oldest, largest, richest, most enterprising, and best organized of its type, and had auxiliary societies throughout the British Isles and Canada."[28]

In 1900–01, the London Society had an income of £46,338 and an expenditure of £36,910 and employed 199 workers at 52 stations, among which 82 of them were converted Jews. "Of the 52 stations 18 are in England, 3 in Austria, 1 in France, 4 in Germany, 2 in Holland, 1 in Italy, 4 in Rumania, 1 in Russia, 1 in Constantinople; in Asia there are 10 stations, among them Jerusalem with 27 workers; in Africa there are 7 stations." Since its foundation, roughly 5,000 Jews were baptized by the Society.[29] In this way, God utilized the Society as a means to fulfill the Bible prophecy since its foundation in 1809.

Later in England, another organization, the Free Church of Scotland Jewish Mission, came to be in 1840. In Ireland, the Presbyterian Church in Ireland Jewish Mission was founded, and in Scotland, the Church of Scotland Jewish Mission, both in 1841. In 1842, the British Society for the Propagation of the Gospel among the Jews came about, followed by many more foundations in 1843, 1854, and 1860, all committed to the sole purpose of proselytizing Jews.[30, 31]

In Germany, the Society for Promoting Christianity among the Jews (Die Gesellschaft zur Verbreitung des Christentums unter den Juden) was founded in 1822 and gave baptism to 713 converted Jews. Since then, more foundations for proselytizing Jews came into existence in 1835, 1836, 1839, 1842, and more. In Switzerland, the first organization was founded in 1830, in France in 1887, and in Scandinavia in 1856.[32, 33]

In Russia, where more than half of world's Jewish population lived, the government limited Protestants from evangelizing Jews and only allowed the state church to handle such missions. Nonetheless, Faltin organized a fruitful mission in 1859 in Kishinef, and Joseph Robinowitz also led a successful undertaking from 1882 to 1899.[34, 35]

In the United States, an independent mission group called the New York City Mission was formed in 1828, which is considered the oldest of all American missions. As for church mission, the Protestant Episcopal made the start with the Church Society for Promoting Christianity amongst the Jews in 1842. Since then, more church missions for evangelizing Jews commenced in 1845, 1871, 1878, and so forth. Such missions to Jews took charge of sending missionaries, publishing tracts, pamphlets, books, and periodicals, and operating the seminaries, schools and hospitals.[36, 37]

The next table summarizes the report given at the First Lutheran Conference on Mission among Israel in Chicago in

1901.[38] The statistics on "workers" in the table includes medical doctors and all others committed to evangelizing the Jews except missioners. Of course, this report is not inclusive of all mission organizations then. Nonetheless, the report reveals how efforts to convert Jews continually spread from Great Britain to other parts of Europe, Australia and even to South Africa.

Organization					
Country	Year	#Station	#Missioner	#Worker	Revenue
The London Society for Promoting Christianity amongst the Jews					
Great Britain	1809	52	45	154	$231,690
The Operative Jewish Converts' Institution					
Great Britain	1831				$3,000
The British Society for Propagation of the Gospel among the Jews					
Great Britain	1842	16	17	4	$30,000
The Jewish Mission of the Presbyterian Church of England					
Great Britain	1860	2	1	2	$7,435
Parochial Missions to the Jews at Home and Abroad					
Great Britain	1875	9	10		$5,000
The Mildmay Mission to the Jews					
Great Britain	1876	9	38		$40,000
The East London Mission to the Jews					
Great Britain	1877	1	8		$14,165
The Barbican Mission to the Jews					
Great Britain	1879	3	4	1	$6,000
The Wild Olive Graft Mission					
Great Britain	1886		3		$1,000
The London City Mission					
Great Britain	1874	1		7	
The Jewish Refugees' Aid Society					
Great Britain	1883				$2,075
The Society for Relief of Persecuted Jews					
Great Britain	1882[39]				
Jerusalem and the East Mission Fund					
Great Britain	1887	5	18		$47,886
The Kilburn Mission to the Jews					
Great Britain	1896		1		$2,350
The Jewish Mission of the Church of Scotland					
Scotland	1841	6	13	16	$27,275

The Ladies' Association for the Education of Jewish Females					
Scotland	1854			23	$6,500
The Jewish Mission of the Free Church of Scotland					
Scotland	1843	5	8	72	$36,830
The Jewish Mission of the United Presbyterian Church					
Scotland	1885				$1,200
The Scotch Home Mission to the Jews					
Scotland	1885				$1,256
The Edinburgh Society for Promoting the Gospel amongst Foreign Jews, Seamen and Immigrants					
Scotland	1891[40]				$1,200
The Jewish Mission of the Presbyterian Church in Ireland					
Ireland	1841	2	6	7	$20,800
The Edzard Fund					
Germany	1667				
The Society for Promoting Christianity among the Jews					
Germany	1822	3	4		$18,000
The Society for Christian Care of Jewish Proselytes					
Germany	1836				$525
The Chief Mission Society of Evangelical Lutherans in Saxony					
Germany	1839				$1,500
The Bavarian Evangelical Lutheran Association for Promoting Christianity among the Jews					
Germany	1849				$550
The Central Association of Evangelical Lutheran Missions among Israel					
Germany	1871	3	3		$3,850
The Wuertenberg Association for Missions among the Jews					
Germany	1874				$925
The Mecklenburg-Schwerin Mission Association among the Jews					
Germany	1886				$163
The Hanoverian Committee for Missions among the Jews					
Germany	1888		1		$500
The Society for Missions to Israel					
Germany	1885		1		$675
Of the Students' Institute Judaica					
Germany	5				
The Rhenish-Westphalian Association for Israel					
Germany	1842	3	3	1	$5,500
The Society of Israel's Friends at Strassburg in Alsace					
Germany	1835				$350
The Society of Friends of Israel in Luebeck					
Germany	1844				$60

The Society of Israel's Friends at Basle					
Switzerland	1830		1		$3,000
The Netherland Society for Promoting Christianity among the Jews					
Netherlands	1844				$1,000
The Netherland Society for Israel					
Netherlands	1861		2		$2,000
The Christian Reformed Mission among the Jews					
Netherlands	1875				$850
The French Society for the Evangelization of Israel					
France	1888		2		$1,250
The Paris Mission to the Jews					
France	1887		1		$1,000
The Central Committee of Missions among Israel					
Norway	1865	2	1	3	$8,500
The Society for Missions to Israel					
Sweden	1876	3	3	3	$10,000
The Evangelical National Society					
Sweden	1889				
The Swedish Missionary Union					
Sweden	1877		1	1	
The Society for Missions to Israel					
Denmark	1885	1	1		$675
The Asylum for Jewish Girls in St. Petersburg					
Russia	1864				$1,400
The Baltic Lutheran Church					
Russia	1865				$1,500
The Lutheran Mission to the Jews at Kishinef					
Russia	1859				$4,500
The Missionary Labor of Joseph Rabinowitch among the Jews of Kishinef					
Russia	1883				
The Church Society for Promoting Christianity among the Jews					
USA	1845	2	5		$20,000
The New York City Mission					
USA	1828[41]				
The Norwegian Lutheran Zion Society in America for the Mission among the Jews					
USA	1878	3	4		$4,000
The Jewish Mission of the Evangelical Lutheran Synod of Missouri, Ohio and other States					
USA	1883	1	1		$1,500
The Hebrew Christian Mission in Chicago					
USA	1885			2	$3,700

The Lutheran Mission among Israel in Chicago					
USA	1893		1		$2,000
Evangelical Lutheran Immanuel Synod in South Australia					
Australia	1867				
Churches in Cape Colony & Basutoland					
South Africa					

Table 1-2. General statistics of missions to the Jews.

Number of Jews Sealed

Let us now shift gears to examine the number of Jews that were converted through these missions. Of all countries, Great Britain poured most resources into converting the Jews. Starting from 1817, the London Society issued Hebrew version of the New Testament.[42]

Although the Jewish population in Britain was comparatively smaller than that in the United States, the missionary works in Britain towards the Jews were vibrant. While only 11 missionary organizations operated in the United States,[43] there were over 28 mission boards with 481 salary paid workers and other unnumbered volunteers in Great Britain toward the close of the nineteenth century. Many mission organizations for Jewish people in Britain also had overseas stations.[44]

In terms of expenses, efforts, and the number of personnel involved, Great Britain was at the forefront of proselytizing the Jews. Towards such missionary activities of churches, the middle class and Jewish immigrants in Great Britain reacted with hostility in the 1860s and 1870s. They feared the extraordinarily zealous proselytizing activities would be similar to Catholics' medieval frenzy that had engendered historical "Inquisition and the Crusades." Eventually, some took antagonism to the streets, attempting to prevent baptism ceremony for the new converts, that police protection was required. Such tension and demonstrative animosity persisted throughout 1890s, during the apogee of "conversionist publishing and missionary activity among Jews."[45]

Historical records reveal the number of baptized Jews during the nineteenth century. Johannes F. A. de le Roi reported that among 204,542 Jewish converts in the nineteenth century, 72,742 became Protestants, 57,300 became Roman Catholics, and 74,500 belonged to Greek Church in Russia. He further reported the average number of Jewish converts amounted to 2,000 per year in the nineteenth century. He also reported that the number increased to 3,000 per year toward the end of the century, with about 1,000 converts per year from Austria-Hungary, 1,000 from Russia, 500 from Germany, and other 500 from Anglo-Saxon.[46]

There are diverse reports on these figures. According to Heman, the nineteenth century converts exceeded 100,000. On the other hand, Salmon wrote in *Handbuch der Mission* (1893) that 130,000 Jews had converted. Another speculated that there were 250,000. According to some sources, there were 40,000 converts between 1836 and 1875 from Russia alone. Johannes F. A. de le Roi reported in *Die Evangelische Christenheit und die Juden* that 50,000 received baptism in England until 1875.[47]

A broadly circulated Hebrew periodical *Hamelitz* published at the end of the nineteenth century wrote, "The majority of Jews are more familiar with the doctrines and sayings of the New Testament than they are with the Talmud and the Pentateuch."[48] The statement bespeaks how vibrant evangelic activities in converting the Jews were at that time.

Medical missions were also in operation in efforts to reach out to Jews. These were measured in "attendances," as an individual patient could make multiple visits. Statistics showed that a patient made five visits to a medical mission center on average. The total attendance counts tallied in England in 1912 from four medical mission centers amounted to 9,600 patients and 48,000 attendances.

Since there were anywhere from six to eleven operative medical missions in any given year in England, the attendance number easily exceeded 100,000 in some years. Judging from the London Society's record of seven medical staff by 1900, the attendance record of Jews must have been very high.[49]

Apart from those recorded to have received baptism, there may also have been some believers who did not outwardly express their faith. Such cases are exemplified in the following excerpt:

> He [an old man] believed passionately in Jesus as the Messiah and Son of God but because he was dependent for support on his son "who is bitterly opposed to Christianity" kept his beliefs secret. Some Jewish converts were sent to the countryside or helped to emigrate to avoid the "stress of persecution."[50]

Various reports and statistics disclose an astonishingly large number of converted Jews during this period, contrary to common prejudices and expectations. Regarding this rare phenomenon, Dr. E. Stock had commented:

> Relatively to the numbers of the Jewish race the converts are as numerous as those from the heathen and much more than those from the Mohammedans. It is estimated that quite 250 Anglican clergymen are converted Jews or the sons of converted Jews. The London Jews Society alone has 93 on its missionary staff . . . Professor Delitzsch estimated that 100,000 Jews had been baptized in the first three-quarters of the nineteenth century.[51]

The *Report of the First Lutheran Conference on Mission among Israel* of 1901 also referenced the statistics on missions to the Jews from 1888, which stated that there were at least 150,000 Jews who embraced Christianity. What is more, the report wrote that the result of evangelizing the Jews is far more favorable than that of evangelizing the heathen world:

> Now then, if through the labors of 400 missionary workers among the Jews 150,000 children of Israel were led directly or indirectly to embrace Christianity, how many heathen, according to the same ratio, should have been brought into the Christian fold by the endeavors of 91,259 missionary workers in heathen lands? Why, 34,313,500. But from the statistics of the last "Ecumenical Missionary Conference" we learn, that the total result of all missionary enterprises in the heathen world during the 19th century is but 4,414,236. The results, therefore, of missionary activity among the Jews are, in spite of the far greater obstacles and hindrances, and in spite also of indolence and aversion on the part of the Christian world, 7¾ times as favorable as those from among the heathen. This I would beg to consider when making comparisons.[52]

In terms of expenses on missions for the Jews, the Berlin Society for Promoting Christianity among the Jews spent 117,152 Reichsthaler to proselytize 461 Jews in fifty years' time. The London Society spent £600 to £3,000 to convert a single Jew from 1863 to 1894.[53]

The proselytization of Jews, albeit costly and laborious, transpired during the nineteenth century along with much goodwill extended to the Jews from the societies and organizations all over the world. This uncommon incident was prophesied in the Bible and was fulfilled just as Revelation writes, that God would seal the foreheads of His servants.

Surely, being born again is a spiritual matter. Therefore, it is probable that not all who outwardly confessed or received baptism became the true children of God. According to the Scripture, there would have been unmistakably 144,000 Jews sealed during this period. The number of converts recorded is between 100,000 and 250,000. It can be assured that a part of the 144,000 is included in these figures. Needless to say, some of the 144,000 may have been saved through the medical missions, while some may have believed in the name of Jesus yet never appeared in statistics. Thus, the statistical reports cannot present accurate numbers. Even so, God is faithful, and He must have fulfilled what He has prophesied.

Anti-Semitism Revival and Zionism

The Industrial Revolution of the nineteenth century also demanded a social reform appropriate for working environment. For the Jews, this meant their rights as laborers were being legally established in many countries for the first time. In 1830, France officially recognized Judaism as a religion. In the German-speaking regions, the Jews were able to conduct businesses as normal citizens with full rights, which was unseen anywhere else. Yet, such social reforms could not prevent the resurgence of anti-Semitism in Germany starting in the middle of the nineteenth century. Such anti-Jewish sentiments revived through two political movements—"Zionism and German unification."[54]

The intent of the latter movement was to unify many German-speaking states into one greater Germany, which did not transpire easily. Zealous nationalist advocators of the movement took their frustration on the Jews for not supporting the unification.[55]

In the mid-nineteenth century, powerful groups that criticized Jewish commercial supremacy and their racial and religious differences surged in French society. As a result, the Anti-Semitic League of France was formed in 1889.[56]

In Russia, Jews were able to enjoy social freedom until Tsar Alexander II (1818–1881) was assassinated in 1881. Many Russians thought the Jews were somehow involved in pulling the strings from behind. Therefore, starting in 1882, the newly enthroned emperor Alexander III (1845–1894) imposed various social restrictions on the Jews. Many Russian Jews were even killed in pogroms throughout early 1880s and early 1900s. Tsar Nicholas II (1868–1918) who began his reign in 1894, blamed Jews for "almost every significant problem." Persecution against Jews was most severe in Russia, where more than half of Jewish population lived.[57]

The Zionist movement, on the other hand, raised different kinds of problems. The ultimate goal of Zionism was to reestablish a nation for the Jewish people, which called for unification and collaboration amongst the Jews from all nations. The movement was a reaction against Christian efforts to proselytize the Jews and was further instigated in response to anti-Semitism in Europe, such as anti-Jewish pogroms in Russia. In 1897, Zionism formally developed into a political movement and encouraged Jewish migration to Palestine, causing new problems for Christian missions. Such political agenda naturally interfered with Christian missions that increasingly drew Jews away from Jewish national roots, but it also depended on moral and material support from Christians to achieve its goals. It was said, "Thus Zionists are enemies of missions, but not enemies of Christianity."[58] As the Zionist movement took off, the conspiracy theories that Jews were intending to conquer the world incited the anti-Semitism all the more.

Despite the presence of persecution during this period, the number of Jews who received baptism increased. For instance, in Prussia, there were 348 baptized in 1888 when anti-Semitism climaxed. This figure was five times the previous years' average annual number, and it slowly declined to 299 by the year 1897. Likewise, in Vienna, the conversions tallied 457 in 1896 and 468 in

1898, which were over 11 times the previous years' average per annum.[59]

The conversion of Jews reached its climax toward the end of the nineteenth century but also begot Zionism and anti-Semitism. Consequently, "the Jews of continental Europe were made to feel that, in spite of their full and hearty participation in the political life and intellectual progress of their country, they were yet regarded and treated as aliens."[60] In this manner, the century of open evangelism to Jews slowly came to a close. The evidence is irrefutable that the Lord had worked in unique ways to bring many Jews to Him from the middle to the end of nineteenth century.

An attempt to proselytize Jews has existed throughout history, but the effort only began to bear fruit in the nineteenth century. The establishment of the London Society in 1809 can be considered the practical onset of the missions. But even the Society failed to erect a Hebrew-Christian Church in 1832. Bear in mind that the interpretation of the sixth seal concluded with the 1833 Sumatra mega-earthquake. The Bible chronicles that "after these things" (Rev 7:1), Jews are sealed. Therefore, the Bible is stating that the sealing of the 144,000 Jews would not occur before 1833.

Obviously, there would have been Jews who got saved before and after the sealing of the 144,000 in Revelation chapter 7. But what God revealed between the sixth and the seventh seal (or the first trumpet) is that He specifically ordained the nineteenth century to bring myriads of Jews to Jesus Christ.

History unfolded as God had spoken: countless mission organizations were formed starting in 1830s over Europe and around the world, and numerous children of Israel came to know Jesus Christ as their Messiah, most plentifully at the end of the nineteenth century and until the beginning of the twentieth century.

CHAPTER 2.
BETWEEN THE SIXTH
AND THE SEVENTH SEALS:
A GREAT MULTITUDE

There are two events in Revelation chapter 7 that are recorded between the sixth and the seventh seals. The second event of the two is described as "a great multitude," as stated in the Scripture below:

> [Rev 7:9] After this I beheld, and, lo, a great multitude, which no man could number, of all nations, and kindreds, and people, and tongues, stood before the throne, and before the Lamb, clothed with white robes, and palms in their hands;
> [Rev 7:10] And cried with a loud voice, saying, Salvation to our God which sitteth upon the throne, and unto the Lamb.
> [Rev 7:11] And all the angels stood round about the throne, and about the elders and the four beasts, and fell before the throne on their faces, and worshipped God,
> [Rev 7:12] Saying, Amen: Blessing, and glory, and wisdom, and thanksgiving, and honour, and power, and might, be unto our God for ever and ever. Amen.

[Rev 7:13] And one of the elders answered, saying unto me, What are these which are arrayed in white robes? and whence came they?

[Rev 7:14] And I said unto him, Sir, thou knowest. And he said to me, These are they which came out of [the] great tribulation, and have washed their robes, and made them white in the blood of the Lamb.

[Rev 7:15] Therefore are they before the throne of God, and serve him day and night in his temple: and he that sitteth on the throne shall dwell among them.

[Rev 7:16] They shall hunger no more, neither thirst any more; neither shall the sun light on them, nor any heat.

[Rev 7:17] For the Lamb which is in the midst of the throne shall feed them, and shall lead them unto living fountains of waters: and God shall wipe away all tears from their eyes.

Who are They, and Where did They Come from?

The multitude appearing in the passage above is already dressed in white robes, made white by washing in the blood of the Lamb. Therefore, they are the New Testament saints who believed in Jesus on earth prior to appearing before the throne of God. In contrast to the fifth seal where the Old Testament believers were given the white robes only after having been slain on earth and crying for revenge under the altar in heaven, the multitude in Revelation chapter 7 are already clothed in white robes and praising God with a loud voice.

At this point, it is important to note that the multitude here is not the raptured people. Scrutinizing the following verse reveals why:

[Rev 7:13] And one of the elders answered, saying unto me, What are these which are arrayed in white robes? and whence came (ἦλθον, ēlthon) they?

The verb "came" in verse 13 is ἦλθον (*ēlthon*) in the second aorist tense in Greek, which is translated as a past tense most of the times. This means that the innumerable multitude was already standing before the throne when John saw them. The following verse shows that even more were being added to the multitude:

[Rev 7:14] And I said unto him, Sir, thou knowest. And he said to me, These are they which came (ἐρχόμενοι, erchomenoi) out of [the] great tribulation, and have washed their robes, and made them white in the blood of the Lamb.

The verb *came* in verse 14 is εϱχομενοι (*erchomenoi*) and is a present participle in Greek, suggesting that people are coming out continually. An accurate translation would write "are coming" rather than "came."[1, 2] In other words, this multitude continues to grow in number as believers who die on earth join the great multitude one by one before the throne of God.[3]

This phenomenon is starkly different from that of the rapture, during which the bodies of saints on earth will undergo changes in the twinkling of an eye and get caught up in the same instant.

[1Co 15:51] Behold, I shew you a mystery; We shall not all sleep, but we shall all be changed,
[1Co 15:52] In a moment, in the twinkling of an eye, at the last trump: for the trumpet shall sound, and the dead shall be raised incorruptible, and we shall be changed.

The rapture will occur collectively in an instant, not over a span of time in a way that it occurs to an individual at a time. Also, in that instant, the raptured will meet the Lord in the air (1Th 4:17) instead of directly appearing before the throne of God. For these reasons, the great multitude in Revelation chapter 7 cannot represent the raptured.

Having established that the multitude does not consist of those raptured, the next question to ask in interpreting this event is "*when* should this event have occurred?" In verse 9, John begins the description of this event with the phrase, "After *this* I beheld," implying that an event has ended and the record of another event is to begin. Knowing what *this* event is and when it is completed would aid in interpreting the timing of the multitude event. Of course, the Scripture makes it clear that *this* event refers to the sealing of the 144,000 Jews, which concluded by the beginning of the twentieth century. Yet, if the multitude event occurred after the sealing of the 144,000 Jews was completed, then the time lapse until the sounding of the first trumpet, World War I in 1914, would be too short for the multitude event to happen.

Closer examination of the Scripture explains this seemingly short duration of the multitude event. When John saw the great multitude, they were already standing before the throne and before the Lamb. The Scripture does not mention when the multitude first started coming up before the throne and the Lamb. In other words, when John saw them in Revelation chapter 7, considerable amount of time had already passed since the first formation of the multitude.

As discussed already, the multitude is an innumerable group of New Testament saints already clothed with white robes. They believed in Jesus while still living on earth, then appeared before the throne and the Lamb after completion of their lives on earth. John witnessed them after they had already appeared before the throne and the Lamb. Their living on earth must have occurred prior to John's witnessing of them before the throne. Thus, John did not account for when the individuals already present before the throne formed the multitude, but could only account for the continual addition of more saints to the multitude.

In conclusion, the exact starting date or time of formation of the multitude cannot be established. Assuming that an average person lived up to seventy or eighty years of age, however, the period when some of the multitude lived on earth may have closely matched the period when the 144,000 Jews were sealed, after 1833 when the sixth seal had finished. Yet this is solely based on the abovementioned assumption. A tentative interpretation on the time of this event is that it occurred during the nineteenth century. Detailed scrutiny on the time of formation of the multitude will be further discussed later.

Like the starting time, the passage in Revelation does not specify the time of completion of the multitude event. This is in contrast with the event of sealing the 144,000 Jews, which concludes before the harming of the land, the sea, and the trees. The fact that there is no clear ending time specified in the Scripture suggests that this multitude event may continue to occur until the time of the rapture. At the time of the rapture, many will be caught up all at once after their bodies are changed into incorruptible ones, but until then, those who fall asleep in Christ having "palms in their hands" come stand before the throne one by one.

At this point, let us read verse 14 again.

> [Rev 7:14] And I said unto him, Sir, thou knowest. And he said to me, These are they which came out of [the] great tribulation (τῆς θλιψεως τῆς μεγαλης, tēs thlipseōs tēs megalēs), and have washed their robes, and made them white in the blood of the Lamb.

The phrase "great tribulation" in this verse has led many to believe that the multitude event would occur during the Daniel's seventieth week, the final seven years before the millennial kingdom. Reading the verse in the original Greek, however, suggests otherwise. While the King James Version translation does not include a definite article in front of "great tribulation," the original Greek definitely includes it and reads, "*the* great tribulation (της θλιψεως της μεγαλης, *tēs thlipseōs tēs megalēs*)."

What is the significance of the presence of a definite article in front of "great tribulation?" Does this "great tribulation" refer to the final seven-year period? Let us first examine what the Lord Himself said regarding this time period:

[Mt 24:21] For then shall be great tribulation (θλῖψις μεγάλη, thlipsis megalē), such as was not since the beginning of the world to this time, no, nor ever shall be.

In this verse, the definite article "the" is not present in front of "great tribulation," but the description "not since the beginning of the world to this time" clearly indicates that the "great tribulation" in the verse refers to the one in the final seven-year period. Let us read another verse in the same passage:

[Mt 24:29] Immediately after the tribulation (τὴν θλῖψιν, tēn thlipsin) of those days shall the sun be darkened, and the moon shall not give her light, and the stars shall fall from heaven, and the powers of the heavens shall be shaken:

Here, Jesus did not use the adjective "great," but in continuation of the same dialogue, a definite article was used to denote the final seven-year period, thus, "the tribulation."

The phrase "great tribulation" in the Bible, however, does not always refer to the final seven-year period. The following is an example:

> [Ac 7:11] Now there came a dearth over all the land of Egypt and Chanaan, and great affliction (θλῖψις μεγάλη, thlipsis megalē): and our fathers found no sustenance.

The "affliction" in this verse comes from the Greek word θλῖψις (thlipsis) which is translated as "tribulation" in other verses. The "great affliction" refers to the great famine experienced at the time of Joseph and does not have a definite article "the" in front. The following is another example:

> [Rev 2:22] Behold, I will cast her into a bed, and them that commit adultery with her into great tribulation (θλῖψιν μεγάλην, thlipsin megalēn), except they repent of their deeds.

This verse is addressed to Thyatira church, warning of great tribulation without the use of the definite article "the." Although the "great tribulation" here may refer to the final seven-year period, the Lord did not specify the nature of the tribulation, did not use a definite article, and did not provide its time limit. Thus, it cannot be concluded that this phrase refers to the final seven years for certain.

The commentaries on "the great tribulation" in Revelation 7:14 vary in opinions. Adam Clarke reinterpreted it as "persecutions of every kind,"[4] and John Gill said, "'the great tribulation,' out of which they came, is not to be restrained to any particular time of trouble, but includes all that has been, is, or shall be; as all the afflictions of the saints."[5]

In accord with other scholars' interpretations, the "great tribulation" may signify a tribulation of great magnitude, not necessarily the one in the final seven-year period. Then what about the definite article "the" in Revelation 7:14? The specificity presented by "the" connotes that the tribulation was mentioned or referred to previously. In this sense, the event is not the one that occurs during the final seven-year period, but rather a tribulation of a large magnitude already made known to the readers. Therefore, historical evidences as well as pertinent verses in the Scriptures should substantiate these points.

In order to understand the nature of the great multitude, let us first find out those who preached the word of God during the nineteenth century. But before further discussion, it should be made clear that the last great tribulation, the persecution by the Antichrist, actually will occur in the latter 3.5 years of the final seven-year period. Details on this topic will be discussed in later volumes.

Charles Spurgeon (1834–1892)

Based on the discussion so far, there may have been a great number of people during the nineteenth century that came to know the Lord while undergoing some kind of tribulation. Let us now examine the history for such a group.

The investigation starts with examining a few servants of the Lord who were instrumental in the nineteenth century: Charles Spurgeon (1834–1892), Dwight L. Moody (1837–1899), George Müller (1805–1898), and James Hudson Taylor (1832–1905).

First of all, Charles Spurgeon, the man known as the "Prince of Preachers" from England, was also famous for his sermons being read more than any other sermons in history. Starting at New Park Street Church in 1854, his congregation exceeded 5,000 through his 38-year ministry there and formed the world's largest independent church at that time. Once, he even preached to more than 20,000 people. At that time, there was no microphone available, but people flooded in to listen to him nevertheless. His sermons were very popular and broadly distributed, as much as 25,000 copies per week in 1865, and translated into more than 20 languages. Throughout his life, he preached to over 10 million people, penned 140 books, and sold over 1 million of his books.[6, 7] In retrospect, the duration of his ministry was from 1854 to 1892.

When Hudson Taylor decided to establish the China Inland Mission (CIM), Spurgeon encouraged Taylor by promoting his mission organization in his publications. Spurgeon also followed George Müller's example in operating an orphanage in Stockwell, England. [8] When Dwight Moody visited England, Spurgeon encouraged Moody and allowed him to preach at his church.[9]

Dwight L. Moody (1837–1899)

D. L. Moody's influence during the nineteenth century was also sensational. He had almost no education background, as he quit his elementary school in the middle, and hence, was poor in grammar. He was not an ordained minister and worked as a shoe salesman. But following his conversion in 1855, he was clearly used by God in a powerful way.[10] In 1860, Moody decided to give up his prosperous sales business and work fulltime for the ministry. Although not having a steady income was a hefty burden to him, he gladly sacrificed all for the Lord.[11]

When he heard of the ministries in England, he desired to benefit from knowing them personally, so he traveled to England in 1867 and met with Charles Spurgeon and George Müller.[12] In 1888, Moody invited Hudson Taylor to the Northfield and Niagara Conferences to preach. This invitation influenced many people to dedicate their lives for Christ and to join Taylor's China Inland Mission. Such non-denominational fellowship and cooperative efforts gave rise to evangelical transatlantic network.[13]

D. L. Moody evangelized about 100 million people in America and Europe from 1860 to 1899. His ministry reduced "the population of hell by a million in doing so."[14]

George Müller (1805–1898)

George Müller is another spiritual giant of the nineteenth century who deserves contemplation. Before his conversion, he was a delinquent. He embezzled his father's government money, loved going to bars and drinking, and played cards until two in the morning even on the very night his mother passed away, unaware of her illness.[15]

When he attended an off-campus Bible study in 1825, he acquainted himself with truly born-again believers and soon entrusted his life to Jesus Christ. In 1829, Müller left Berlin for London for missions, and in 1830, he accepted the offer to be a minister at a small congregation for a salary of £55 per year.[16]

Afterwards, he declared to the brethren with the reading of Philippians chapter 4 that he would relinquish any regular salary, but rather solely rely on small or big voluntary contributions from donors who would give anonymously, for God is pleased with cheerful givers and honors every penny from the poor. This way, Müller put up a box in the chapel and relied on gifts God provided through saints who were moved by the Spirit and desired to support his cause. At the same time, he determined not to ask any man, not even his brethren and sisters, to help supplement his expenses on account of Lord's service.[17]

In 1832, Müller relocated to Bristol for ministry. In 1834, he and his friend Henry Craik founded the Scriptural Knowledge Institution (SKI) to support missionaries at home and abroad, to distribute Bibles and religious tracts, and to provide day schools and Sunday schools to the elderly and children.[18] Through the SKI, he disbursed "285,407 Bibles, 1,459,506 New Testaments, and 244,351 other religious texts, which were translated into twenty other languages." Müller also utilized the institution as a channel to provide for other "faith missionaries," including those in Hudson Taylor's China Inland Mission. Müller was an example for Taylor to follow, and Taylor visited Müller in 1865 for prayer and guidance.[19]

In 1836, George Müller began an orphanage at a house he rented for himself, with a capacity of 30 children.[20] Since its initiation, "George Müller cared for 10,000 orphaned children in Bristol during the 19th century. He never made appeals for money, trusting implicitly in God, he received £1,500,000 in answer to prayer. At present day prices, this would be well over £86,000,000."[21]

From 1875, when he reached the age of seventy, he traveled to various places in the world on missions for seventeen years. He toured "the United States of America four times, India twice and on three occasions toured Australia and the Colonies. In addition, George Müller preached in 42 countries, including China and Japan." His travel covered 200,000 miles in all in times before the advent of cars and airplanes, and he preached to over 3 million people during his missionary travel.[22]

George Müller was truly a man of prayer. One famous real illustration of an answer to his prayer says:

> "The children are dressed and ready for school. But there is no food for them to eat," the housemother of the orphanage informed George Mueller. George asked her to take the 300 children into the dining room and have them sit at the tables. He thanked God for the food and waited. George knew God would provide food for the children as He always did. Within minutes, a baker knocked on the door. "Mr. Mueller," he said, "last night I could not sleep. Somehow I knew that you would need bread this morning. I got up and baked three batches for you. I will bring it in." Soon,

there was another knock at the door. It was the milkman. His cart had broken down in front of the orphanage. The milk would spoil by the time the wheel was fixed. He asked George if he could use some free milk. George smiled as the milkman brought in ten large cans of milk. It was just enough for the 300 thirsty children.[23]

James Hudson Taylor (1832–1905)

During the early childhood years of Hudson Taylor, Britain was in turmoil due to the First Opium War (1839–1842) with China. In 1841, China had ceded Hong Kong to Britain, and in 1842, the five ports—Shanghai, Canton, Ningpo, Fuchow, and Amoy—were opened as a result. In 1849, Taylor repented and turned to the Lord at his age of seventeen.[24] That following year, Taiping Rebellion (1850–1864) began in China.

Under the auspices of the Chinese Evangelization Society, Taylor left for China in 1853 and landed in 1854 in the midst of Taiping Rebellion. In 1855, he had a chance to explore China's inland and was exposed to the tangible needs of the place. Encouraged by George Müller's letter to live by faith, Taylor resigned from the Chinese Evangelical Society in 1856 to be independent. In 1858, in Ningpo he married Maria Dyer, but returned to England in 1860 due to his dire health problems.[25]

In 1865, Taylor founded the China Inland Mission (CIM) and recruited twenty-four volunteer missionaries. Charles Spurgeon then was also deeply touched by Taylor's passion for China. Taylor left London and arrived in Shanghai in 1866 with other missionaries. [26] Twenty-four missionaries dispersed in four stations labored all together in planting churches. Different from other missionaries of the time, Taylor's team dressed in Chinese attire to assimilate to Chinese custom. These are Taylor's words:

"Let us in everything not sinful become like the Chinese, that by all means we may save some."[27]

In 1868, his mission compound in Yangchow was attacked and plundered, and individuals suffered injuries, but Taylor refused to take legal measures to retaliate or to be compensated. A distorted version of rumor spread in England, denigrating Taylor's reputation and dignity. Nevertheless, George Müller continued to support Taylor in good faith.[28]

During his missions, Taylor lost his children, and was bereaved of his wife by cholera in 1870, the same year the massacre in Tianjin erupted. In 1871, Taylor had to return to England to care for his health and married his second wife, Jennie Faulding. In 1872 in a Bible Conference, Dwight Moody heard Taylor preach. Later that year, Taylor departed to China again with his new wife.[29]

In 1876, the signing of the Chefoo Convention settled diplomatic issues between England and China, opening the inland China to evangelism. In 1885, "The Cambridge Seven" joined missionaries in China. Fourteen more missionaries headed to China with Taylor after his only trip to America in 1888, when he preached at Moody's Northfield Conference and few other places.[30]

The missions expanded continually, and by 1905, the CIM statistics showed there were total of "849 missionaries, including missionaries' wives and associates, with 1,282 native workers; 205 stations, and 632 sub-stations, and 35,726 communicants; 188 schools, with nearly 3,000 pupils, and 44 hospitals and dispensaries."[31] "During his 51 years of service there, his China Inland Mission . . . developed a witnessing Chinese church of 125,000. It has been said at least 35,000 were his own converts and that he baptized some 50,000."[32]

As examined above, the four men of God from the nineteenth century set good examples, followed in one another's footsteps, and supported each other when in need with aids and encouragement.

Such mutual brotherly love is exemplified in the *Wordless Book* created by Charles Spurgeon in 1866. The original design consisted of three colors of black, red, and white. Spurgeon said:

> The old minister used to gaze upon the black leaf to remind himself of his sinful state by nature, upon the red leaf to call to his remembrance the precious blood of Christ, and upon the white leaf to picture to him the perfect righteousness which God has given to believers through the atoning sacrifice of Jesus Christ his Son.[33]

Then in 1875, D. L. Moody added the color gold after white to the *Wordless Book* to represent "the glories of Heaven." Hudson Taylor adopted this addition and used it effectively in his ministries in China.[34] It is needless to say the *Wordless Book* proved potent in China where there were many illiterates. Therefore, the evolvement of the *Wordless Book* highlights how the brethren learned from one another and encouraged each other to reap greater harvests.

The mutual brotherly love and the work among these servants of Lord are representative of the following Scripture:

> [Eph 4:11] and *he* has given some *apostles*, and some prophets, and some *evangelists*, and some shepherds and *teachers*,
> [Eph 4:12] for the perfecting of the saints; with a view to [the] work of [the] *ministry*, with a view to the edifying of the body of Christ;
> [Eph 4:13] until we all arrive at the unity of the faith and of the knowledge of the Son of God, at [the] full-

grown man, at [the] measure of the stature of the fulness of the Christ; (Darby)

Hudson Taylor served a role of an apostle; Dwight L. Moody was a powerful evangelist; Charles Spurgeon was a renowned teacher; and George Müller dedicated for the work of the ministry. As a result, the church benefited from their services and grew stronger in unity of faith and in mutual edification.

During the time of Hudson Taylor's ministry, China was politically very unstable. When he first landed in 1854, the Taiping Rebellion was already in progress. From 1855 to the end of the 19th century, many rebellions, riots, and massacres as well as Second Opium War occurred. In 1899, the Boxer Society was formed, laying the foundation for the following year's Boxer Uprising, which was supported by Empress Dowager Cixi's issue of an anti-foreign decree that officially declared war against European powers. At the turn of the twentieth century, the Imperial Decree ordered murdering of all foreigners.[35]

Protestant Missions in China

Hudson Taylor was not the only one who contributed to the missions in China. Protestant missions in China were started in 1807 by a Presbyterian missionary Robert Morrison (1782–1834) from England. He translated the Bible into Chinese and dedicated himself to "social transformation of Chinese culture through Christian education."[36]

Robert Morrison's endeavor to indigenize Christianity in China came to fruition when converts devoted to the ministry of translation, printing, and distributing Bibles and tracts. One of the most faithful pupils of Morrison was Liang Fa, who later became the first Chinese Protestant minister and continued to evangelize throughout his life. Unfortunately, one of the side effects was that Liang Fa's writings affected Hong Xiuquan, the leader of Taiping

Rebellion, who considered himself as Jesus' younger brother, to have the "apocalyptic vision of national salvation."[37] Taiping Rebellion left "a death toll 30 times greater than that of the contemporaneous American Civil War."[38]

At the dawn of the nineteenth century, the mission works in China were naturally limited to the areas that foreigners were allowed to stay and travel within. But when such restrictions were lifted, the number of foreign mission workers began to soar to 2,500 in 1900, counting wives and children.[39]

When China lost its war against the Western colonial powers, unequal treaties were signed between the Qing dynasty of China and the Western forces. Although this furnished an opportune momentum for missionary activities in China, the successful mission enterprises by the foreigners were interpreted by Chinese nationalists as an "indisputable evidence that Christian mission was the tool of Western cultural imperialism." Therefore, the growth of Christianity in China instigated anti-Christian riots and animosity, which manifested in different forms of harassment.[40]

The extreme manifestation of this anti-Christian sentiment was the Boxer Uprising in 1900.[41] During this uprising, 189 foreign Protestant missionaries were killed. Among them, the largest loss was suffered by the China Inland Mission, having lost 58 missionaries and 21 children in all. Chinese Christians were also targeted during the anti-Christian movement; thousands of them were put to death between 1898 and 1900.[42, 43]

As a result, in the China Centenary Missionary Conference of 1907, expansion of various Christian enterprises in "educational, medical, and other social dimensions of mission" was emphasized. As civilization, social services, and education are no substitute for the gospel, preaching, and spirituality, the aftermath of viewing them with equal importance did not result in a synergistic outcome but secularization, professionalism, and elitism of mission enterprises.[44]

Protestant Missions in Other Countries

The table below lists the countries or regions where the gospel was preached since the time of William Carey (1761–1834) and throughout the nineteenth century. [45] If missionaries were dispatched into a single country over multiple years, only the first year of the dispatch has been noted.

Year	Country/Region
1793	India, New South Wales
1796	Pacific Islands (Tahiti)
1789	South Africa (Zulus)
1804	West Africa (Sierra Leone)
1806	Ceylon
1807	China (Hong Kong)
1813	Java, West Indies, Burma
1814	New Zealand
1815	Levant (Malta)
1818	Madagascar
1819	Syria, Egypt, Hawaiian Islands
1820	South Africa (Cape Colony)
1821	West Africa (Liberia)
1828	Greece, Siam
1829	Persia
1830	East Africa (Abyssinia)
1831	Turkey (Constantinople)
1832	Mauritius
1834	South Africa (Bechuanas)
1835	Australia
1836	Borneo, South America (Argentina)
1838	Malaysia
1839	New Hebrides
1840	Madras

1844	East African Coast, South America (Tierra del Fuego)
1846	West Africa (Gold Coast)
1847	West Africa (Angola), West Africa (Congo), Melanesia
1849	Central America (Mosquito Coast)
1852	Palestine, Micronesia
1855	Ladakh (Little Tibet)
1856	Dutch East Indies, South America (Colombia)
1857	Bulgaria, West Africa (Nigeria)
1859	Japan
1861	Straits Settlements, East Africa (Mombasa)
1862	Sumatra, Australasia, West Africa (Senegambia)
1865	Formosa
1868	German Southwest Africa
1869	South America (Brazil)
1870	Mongolia, Mexico
1871	New Guinea
1874	British East Africa, British Central Africa, Congo Free State, Turkey (Greeks)
1880	Portuguese West Africa (Benguella)
1881	Algeria
1882	Central America (Guatemala)
1883	East Equatorial Africa
1884	Korea
1886	Arabia (Aden), German East Africa
1888	South America (Paraguay)
1889	West Africa (Gabun)
1890	Arabia (Bahrein)
1899	Philippines, Porto Rico, W.I.

Table 2-1. Protestant missions in the nineteenth century.

Before the time of William Carey, Protestant missions were practically non-existent other than those led by Moravian Church. But since William Carey, the "father of modern missions," the gospel was carried to all corners of the world in the nineteenth century by numerous Christians who wanted to obey the Lord's Great Commission and make disciples of all nations. This period full of great missionary achievements was thus labeled by historian Kenneth Scott Latourette as "the Great Century," [46] because more was achieved in one century than all previous eras combined.

The Great Tribulation

So far, the history of how Christianity expanded globally in the nineteenth century has been examined. Finally, let us deliberate on what "[the] great tribulation" in Revelation 7:14 means. As discussed before, this does not refer to the tribulation during the final seven years. Rather, the tribulation can be understood as any persecution that has persisted throughout history wherever the gospel has spread.

Even in the lives of Hudson Taylor and the missionaries of the CIM, such tribulation accompanied them all throughout their missions. The fury did not stop at persecuting the foreign missionaries but extended even onto the native Chinese believers who accepted the gospel then. Records show that a few thousand Chinese Christians lost lives during the Boxer Uprising. However, it is more likely that there was more persecution than what was recorded in history. Therefore, many more Chinese believers might have been persecuted during the wide spreading of gospel at the time.

> [1Th 1:6] And ye became followers of us, and of the Lord, having received the word in much *affliction*, with joy of the Holy Ghost:

The New Testament also speaks of much affliction that other followers of the Lord suffered. The Bible consistently warns the saints that persecution will follow where the good news is received with eagerness.

If this is the case, in what areas will saints suffer persecution? Could tribulation be limited to regions where the gospel reaches for the first time? Certainly not. Correspondingly, Albert Barnes commented about "[the] great tribulation" of Revelation 7:14 as follows:

> The word rendered "tribulation" — θλίψις thlipsis — is a word of general character, meaning "affliction," though perhaps there is here an allusion to persecution. The sense, however, would be better expressed by the phrase "great trials." The object seems to have been to set before the mind of the apostle a view of those who had suffered much, and who by their sufferings had been sanctified and prepared for heaven, in order to encourage those who might be yet called to suffer.[47]

In this sense, not only Hudson Taylor but also Charles Spurgeon, Dwight L. Moody, George Müller, plus all other partakers of evangelism matured in Christ through the great tribulation. An innumerable number of saints who came before them also received much affliction in obedience to the faith and with joy of the Holy Spirit.

Then what sets the great tribulation in Revelation 7:14 as "the" one? The definite article "the" indicates that the great tribulation had been referred to before. When was it addressed? Indeed, it was the Lord who had spoken of the tribulation. Jesus foretold the saints that His followers will face tribulation in this world.

[Jn 16:33] These things I have spoken unto you, that in me ye might have peace. In the world ye shall have *tribulation*: but be of good cheer; I have overcome the world.

This tribulation was forewarned not only by Jesus but also by the apostles.

[Ac 14:22] Confirming the souls of the disciples, and exhorting them to continue in the faith, and that we must through much *tribulation* enter into the kingdom of God.

According to the Scripture, whoever loves the Lord and pursues the life of His true discipleship will be persecuted and face tribulation. This must be the tribulation allotted to those who walk faithfully in obedience to and in love for the Lord.

[1Th 2:14] For ye, brethren, became followers of the churches of God which in Judaea are in Christ Jesus: for ye also have *suffered* like things of your own countrymen, even as they have of the Jews:

When tribulation comes, saints suffer. There may be different degrees of suffering, but the nature of tribulation is alike, for the purpose of tribulation is to mold the saints to be Christ-like.

[Ro 5:3] And not only so, but we glory in *tribulations* also: knowing that *tribulation* worketh patience;
[Ro 5:4] And patience, experience; and experience, hope:

Let us now ask, if the saints in Revelation 7:9 are those who went through the tribulation, what do the palms in their hands signify? A palm tree is characterized by a long singular stem with its branches at the top that typify victory.[48] Read the following peculiar characteristics of palm tree: "the palm tree being of such a nature, as is reported, that the more weight is hung upon it, the higher it rises, and the straighter it grows."[49]

To understand the significance of the palms, let us examine the following Scripture where palms appear:

> [Lev 23:40] And ye shall take you on the first day the boughs of goodly trees, branches of *palm* trees, and the boughs of thick trees, and willows of the brook; and ye shall rejoice before the LORD your God seven days.

The Scripture above instructs how to celebrate the Feast of Tabernacles, which signifies the Lord's dwelling with the saints after the victory of the final war, the battle of Armageddon, upon His return. The verse shows that the branches of palm tree relate to victory and rejoicing.

Therefore, in Revelation 7:9, the palms are in the saints' hands in expression of joy after all the tribulations they have gone through and for victories achieved by walking with their Lord.

The multitude standing before the throne and the Lamb are certainly not limited to people from the nineteenth century only. They must include all Christians from the New Testament age who not only believe in the Lord that died on the cross for them but also are found victorious. This multitude grows in number even to this day. The souls will praise the Lord as one group before the throne and the Lamb until their bodies are resurrected at the time of the rapture.

Finally, why did God show a great multitude between the sixth and the seventh seals? Undoubtedly, it is because the nineteenth century is when the gospel was spread widely throughout the world. It was indeed the century when many believers of "all nations, kindreds, people, and tongues" came forth to His throne. In the regions where the gospel was first reached, there were tribulations. Yet, regardless of the duration of the gospel's influence in a region, it is God's desire that His saints be molded into His likeness and mature in their walks with Him through the tribulation. Showing the multitude with palms in their hands at the time of the nineteenth century thereby encourages other followers from conventionally Christian nations to also take the Lord's yoke and be found as victors coming out of the tribulation with palms in their hands.

CHAPTER 3.
THE THIRD TRUMPET:
THE STAR CALLED WORMWOOD

The first volume of the series revealed that the seals in Revelation had occurred in centurial intervals. Similarly, history reveals how the trumpets in Revelation occur in decadal intervals. If the trumpets do occur in decadal intervals, then the trumpet events will be much easier to identify and match with the corresponding incidents in history than those of the seals.

Due to the fact that finding concrete historical evidence, such as hard data and primary research accounts, for the seals is relatively harder, the interpretations on the seven seals may be subject to room for error. In contrast, finding evidence for interpreting the trumpets can be relatively easier for obvious reasons. They occurred more recently, abound in historical accounts and archives, and have occurred in much shorter time intervals.

So in interpreting the trumpets, it is simplest to first identify the easiest event to interpret. If the obviously most easily identifiable trumpet event is interpreted first, it will make the rest of the interpretations much easier. God could have provided names of some events so that they are easily identified. Specific names would serve as definite clues in interpreting the trumpet events.

Among the seven trumpets, there are not many specifics provided for the seventh trumpet other than lightnings, voices, thunderings, an earthquake, and great hail. Among the remaining six trumpets, the events provided with the names or description of a person or object are the following three events: the third trumpet for which the name Wormwood is introduced, the fifth trumpet for which the names Abaddon and Apollyon appear, and the sixth trumpet revolving around the Euphrates river.

Beginning with the interpretation on the third trumpet, let us look into Revelation chapter 8, where the name *Wormwood* is found:

> [Rev 8:10] And the third angel sounded, and there fell a great star from heaven, burning as it were a lamp, and it fell upon the third part of the rivers, and upon the fountains of waters;
> [Rev 8:11] And the name of the star is called *Wormwood*: and the third part of the waters became wormwood; and many men died of the waters, because they were made bitter.

The most important event to note here is that something fell from the sky. Then, it affected the rivers and the fountains of water. Consequently, the waters became "wormwood." The word *wormwood* means bitter. Because the water turned bitter, people died from the waters. The key elements here are the "rivers" and the "waters."

Let us first reason with the given descriptions in the passage. It writes that many men died from drinking the water, because the water was contaminated with something. What might be the contaminant?

Could the contaminant be some poisonous chemical substance? Probably not. If one heard news that some neighbors died from drinking the water, would he drink the same water? He would most naturally install a water purifier and be immune to dying from drinking the water. Conversely, not many people would have died from water if the pollutant in question were chemical substances. Given the modern-day advancement in water filtering technology, hardly anyone would die from drinking it.

What then are some contaminants that cannot be filtered by water purifier? If there is one, it would be radioactive rays. Perhaps some high-tech filters could screen out radioactive elements like cesium, but certainly not the radioactive rays emitted from the elements. Moreover, the radiation would contaminate the water molecules even before any of the radioactive substances is filtered. Consequently, even if radioactive substances are filtered, people would die because the water would turn "bitter."

Another interesting thing to note from the passage is the *singular* star, which fell on many rivers and lakes. How could one entity fragmentize into many particles? If they fell in many rivers and fountains of water, then it suggests that some radioactive substance initially of one lump must have atomized into fine pieces later.

What is more, how did they come down from the sky? In order for small particulate matters suspended in the atmosphere to fall, some form of precipitation is required. Therefore, these following conditions occurring together may fulfill the third trumpet event: some radioactive lump ascends to the sky, spreads to wide regions via wind currents, and the fine radioactive particles rain down to contaminate many rivers and lakes. How would radioactive materials end up in the sky? Surmising from the description "burning as it were a lamp," there may have been some nuclear power plant explosion.

Chernobyl Nuclear Power Plant Disaster

The scientific name for *Wormwood* is *Artemisia vulgaris* (mugwort or common wormwood).[1] In Ukrainian, mugwort is called chornobyl. In Russian, chornobyl is translated as chernobyl.

The name chornobyl has an interesting history, as it means "place where mugwort grows" in the related Indo-European languages.[2]

An incident called Chernobyl disaster happened in the days of Soviet Union. Perhaps many readers are aware of this famous incident. When God wrote about Wormwood, He was foretelling and hinting to mankind that this third trumpet is about the Chernobyl Nuclear Power Plant disaster. Needless to say, it must be examined if the substances that fell from Chernobyl disaster upon the rivers turned waters into bitter wormwood and caused people to die from drinking it.

The Chernobyl nuclear disaster occurred on April 26, 1986. When it did, four hundred times more radioactive material was released than that of the atomic bombing of Hiroshima.[3] Although it is not possible to know how many died from the Chernobyl incident, the resultant devastation was overwhelming. A Greenpeace video filmed after twenty years of the accident testifies that there were "76 dead cities, towns, and villages" in all.[4]

Kofi Annan, the former Secretary-General of the United Nations, also assessed: "At least 3 million children in Belarus, Ukraine and the Russian Federation require physical treatment [due to the Chernobyl accident]." Likewise, Angelina Nyagu, a member of an organization by the name of Physicians of Chernobyl attested: "Today, more than seven million people are suffering due to the Chernobyl disaster . . . There is no precedent in the history of mankind."[5]

A scientific journal listed in PubMed, the database of which is maintained by the United States National Library of Medicine at the National Institutes of Health, reveals that the concentration of the Chernobyl radionuclides in the Northern Hemisphere is sometimes found "100,000 times more than the local background level." Among the list of affected things are "sediments, water, plants, and animals." The journal writes that the "air particulate activity over all of the Northern Hemisphere reached its highest levels since the termination of nuclear weapons testing— sometimes up to 1 million times higher than before the Chernobyl contamination."[6]

Many Men Died of the Waters

Let us be reminded that mainly water was affected by this nuclear disaster, as in Revelation 8:11:

[Rev 8:11] And the name of the star is called Wormwood: and the third part of the *waters* became wormwood; and many men died of the *waters*, because they were made bitter.

Revelation clearly talks about the water contamination as the primary cause of death. However, some online resources do not reveal how seriously the waters were affected. The Wikipedia page on the Chernobyl disaster even miswrites that the level of radioactivity in rivers and reservoirs was generally below guideline limits for safe drinking water. It even says that groundwater was not badly affected by the Chernobyl accident since radionuclides with short half-lives decayed away long before they could affect groundwater supplies.[7]

The report on the accident by the Soviet Union was not reliable,[8] perhaps because they did not want to take upon the responsibility to compensate for the nuclear disaster. Therefore, it is important to also review the research investigations released from private and foreign groups, who act as third party to this matter.

A film was produced by NHK, titled *Chernobyl, the Bitter Taste of Wormwood*. In it, Japanese investigators traced the radioactive contamination of water that affected the food chain, caused cancers, and killed many people.[9] It is interesting that these

Japanese investigators also knew that Chernobyl means wormwood, as the title of their film indicates. Their interpretation is significantly supportive of the interpretation that the third trumpet was actually realized as written in Revelation.

The NHK report, one of the most sought and viewed videos on the accident, clearly testifies to the seriousness of water contamination. According to the video, the accident was detected in the sky by a US satellite, which captured the red burning nuclear reactor that was heated up from malfunction.[10]

After the day of the accident, April 26, the radionuclides quickly spread. A minimum of 300 million curies of radioactive particles shot up into the clouds upon the Chernobyl explosion. "In southern Germany, for example, radioactive fallout was five times greater than during the period of twelve years when the nuclear weapons were tested." Computer simulation shows that, within two days, it reached the Scandinavian Peninsula. Within ten days, the whole Soviet Union and the Far East were affected.[11]

The environmental damage was very serious because it rained for many days after the accident. Rainy clouds heavily deposited with the radioactive particles were widely dispersed with high-altitude winds. Then as the rain poured down, many radioactive hotspots were created.[12]

The NHK reporters compared the map of the hotspots published by the Swedish Meteorological and Hydrological Institute with the rainfall records during the days that followed the Chernobyl accident. The investigation revealed the radiation contamination was exceptionally high where precipitation was heavy.[13]

In a small Swedish town near Älvkarleby, 1,200 kilometers away from Chernobyl, the radioactivity detector responded outdoors eight times higher than indoors of a resident's house. The NHK team commented:

If we are to accept the Soviet report, it also meant that the contamination here was 10 times greater than Kiev, a city of 130 km away from Chernobyl . . . Rain had generated the hotspot. This map published by Swedish organization shows the pattern of radioactive fallout in the country. The area colored dark red from Gavle north to Sundsvall marks the hotspot. We found the perfect fit when we compare it with the rainfall records for the 29th of April. The greater the rainfall, the greater the radioactivity.[14]

There, extraordinary levels of radioactivity were detected in the wayside of paved roads as the rainfalls drifted off the surface onto the side of the pavement. Compared to wooden areas which also showed high level of radioactivity, radioactivity reading was a few times higher in the roadside, a little distant from the pavement, which ranged above one rem, which is "more than double the maximum permissible level of the annual exposure for the general public . . . It appears that here too rain had an effect. Because the paved surface of the road does not soak up the water, rain water had gathered by the wayside, so that exceptionally high count of radiation had built up."[15]

About the meteorological relationship between the rain and the radioactivity, the Swedish Meteorological and Hydrological Institute analyzed it in this way:

> The altitude to which fission products were carried at Chernobyl was in the region of 2,000 m. At this level, rain clouds form, and the rainout washout effect results. [According to Meteorologist Mr. C. Persson,] "It is caused by the precipitation. When the rain is created in the clouds, some part of radioactivity can be included in the raindrops up in the clouds. Also when the rain falls down, the contaminated air below the

clouds can be washed out, and another radioactivity is deposited on the ground as a result of the rain."[16]

The government of Turkey was worried about the possible contamination of the Black Sea. "It might develop into a serious international issue apart from worrying effects on marine life. The coverage team obtained data of the Black Sea that has been gathered jointly by oceanographers from five countries including the Unites States. Water samples were taken near the surface at seven points in the Black Sea. At one point, cesium contamination was about 40 times greater than in clean waters of the north Atlantic. Sea currents indicated that the contaminated water had originated along the Bulgarian coast: the result of direct fallout of particles onto the sea surface."[17]

The NHK video also summarized the findings from the Soviet report to the International Atomic Energy Agency on the number of future cancer patients linked to the accident: "Less than 5,000 through direct exposure, 1,500 by drinking contaminated milk, and another 38,000 by contaminated food, giving a grand total of over 44,000."[18] As mentioned previously, the Soviet report seemed to downscale the effects of the accident.

Just as the Soviet report addressed the problem of internal exposure through radioactive foods, the NHK team raised concern and stated:

> About 200 million people including victims of Soviet Union have already been exposed to external radiation of Chernobyl origin. Internal exposure is expected to increase as more people come into contact with contaminated foods: fresh water fish, fruits, berries, and nuts. It must be taken into account this biological concentration of radioactive contaminants.[19]

In sum, the NHK report conclusively testified the water contamination as the primary source of sickness and death.

The Scripture specifies that the *third part* of the waters became wormwood. The *National Geographic* documentary on Chernobyl accident stated:

> The press described the Chernobyl as an apocalypse . . . Nothing like this has ever happened before. Radioactive fuel fragments explode directly into the atmosphere. Investigators calculate they shoot more than half a mile into the sky. Some of the radioactive material is light enough to be carried by the wind, and spreads over thousands of miles. Within ten days it reaches as far as Japan and North America.[20]

The research findings testify that the radioactive material not only spread throughout Russia but also to China and Japan in the east, parts of Europe, the Scandinavian Peninsula, and the Americas in the northwest. In sum, the regions contaminated by the radioactive nuclides from Chernobyl reached the third of world's water sources.

Is It an Actual Star?

The question still remained, however, whether the Scripture was referring to an actual star falling from heaven rather than the fireball from an explosion. Thus, the Scripture was further scrutinized.

> [Rev 8:10] And the third angel sounded, and there fell a great star from heaven, *burning* (καίω, *kaiō*) as it were a *lamp* (Λαμπάς, *lampas*), and it fell upon the

third part of the rivers, and upon the fountains of waters;

In the Chernobyl nuclear accident, there was a great fire rising to the sky that was indeed "burning (καίω, *kaio*) as it were a lamp (λαμπάς, *lampas*)." The documentary from *National Geographic* explains:

> Explosion is an imprecise word. It was like a volcanic eruption . . . The blast generates the huge force of pressure against the reactor's 2,000 ton lid. Eight tons of highly radioactive debris explodes into the sky. Nothing like this has ever happened before.[21]

Returning to the Scripture again, it reads:

[Rev 8:10] . . . there fell a great star from heaven . . .
[Rev 8:10] . . . ἔπεσεν ἐκ τοῦ οὐρανοῦ ἀστὴρ μέγας (*epesen ek tou ouranou astēr megas*) . . .

The verb "fell" ἔπεσεν (*epesen*) here comes from the root word πίπτω (*piptō;* to fall). The preposition ἐκ (*ek*) means: "out of, from, by, away from, etc."[22] "Τοῦ οὐρανοῦ" (*tou ouranou;* of [the] heaven) is the genitive form of "ὁ οὐρανός" (*ho ouranos;* the heaven), ἀστὴρ (*astēr*) is a noun meaning "star," and μέγας (*megas*) is an adjective meaning "large."

The preposition ἐκ (*ek*) is used to point out an "origin," but ἐκ (*ek*) also expresses "coming out of/from" the original place or location.[23]

To determine the nature of the star and its origin, the Scripture can be examined where the word ἀστὴρ (*astēr;* star) is used. Among the twenty-four uses of the word ἀστὴρ (*astēr;* star) in the Scripture, the expression "star from heaven" especially demands closer look.

In the case of the sixth seal, there were stars that fell from the sky. History revealed the event corresponded to the Leonids meteor shower. Then, what words were used to describe the falling stars?

> [Rev 6:13] And *the stars of heaven fell* unto the earth, even as a fig tree casteth her untimely figs, when she is shaken of a mighty wind.
> [Rev 6:13] . . . οἱ ἀστέρες τοῦ οὐρανοῦ ἔπεσαν (*hoi asteres tou ouranou epesan*) . . .

The word ἔπεσαν (*epesan*; fell) here is the second aorist form of πίπτω (*piptō*; to fall). While τοῦ οὐρανοῦ (*tou ouranou*; of [the] heaven) is written in genitive form of the noun heaven, the preposition ἐκ (*ek*; out of/from) is not attached in front of heaven as in "ἐκ τοῦ οὐρανοῦ" (*ek tou ouranou*; from [the] heaven) in Revelation 8:10.

In other words, the stars described in Revelation 6:13 are the actual "stars of the sky," not "stars (flying in) from the sky" as in Revelation 8:10. This shows that the preposition ἐκ (*ek*) is not necessary to describe the celestial bodies originally belonging to heaven. Consequently, interpreting the word "stars" as meteors is justified in all aspects in Revelation 6:13.

Let us now examine the description of the fall of Satan:

> [Lk 10:18] And he said unto them, I beheld *Satan* as lightning *fall from heaven*.
> [Lk 10:18] . . . τὸν Σατανᾶν (*ton Satanan*) . . . ἐκ τοῦ οὐρανοῦ πεσόντα (*ek tou ouranou pesonta*)

In this passage where Satan falls, the term ἐκ (*ek*) is used. Although Satan was in heaven before falling, he does not belong to heaven nor originate from heaven. Therefore, Satan's description does not merely use the genitive form "τὸν Σατανᾶν τοῦ οὐρανοῦ" (*ton Satanan tou ouranou;* Satan of [the] heaven). If there were no ἐκ (*ek*) and only genitive form were used, it would signify that Satan pertains to heaven. However, the presence of ἐκ (*ek*) clearly designates that Satan somehow ended up in heaven before falling down like lightning, but inherently by no means belonged to heaven.

Lastly, let us look at another passage where the word ἀστὴρ (*astēr;* star) is used:

> [Rev 12:4] And his tail drew the third part of the *stars of heaven* (ἀστέρων τοῦ οὐρανοῦ, *asterōn tou ouranou*), and did cast them to the earth: and the dragon stood before the woman which was ready to be delivered, for to devour her child as soon as it was born.

In this case, although a genitive expression without the preposition ἐκ (*ek*) is used, the "stars of [the] heaven" might not represent actual stars observed at night, but instead angelic beings or, less likely, once eminent human teachers,[24] as they are "cast to the earth." If they were actual stars, how could the "third part of the stars of heaven" be cast down to planet Earth at once? Therefore, the "stars" in this passage are allegorical, yet the genitive expression without ἐκ (*ek*) still conveys that they are the angels pertaining to heaven.

Now, let us return to discussion of the ἀστὴρ (*astēr;* star) in the third trumpet.

> [Rev 8:10] . . . fell a great star from heaven . . .
> [Rev 8:10] . . . ἔπεσεν ἐκ τοῦ οὐρανοῦ ἀστὴρ μέγας (*epesen ek tou ouranou astēr megas*) . . .

The "great star" of the third trumpet may or may not be a real star of heavenly origin. If the Scripture was written without the preposition ἐκ (*ek*) as in "ἔπεσεν ἀστὴρ μέγας τοῦ οὐρανοῦ" (*epesen astēr megas tou ouranou*; fell a great star of [the] heaven), then one could assure that the "great star" in question is an actual celestial body. However, the use of the preposition ἐκ (*ek*) together with the genitive form of heaven translates as "from heaven" and further increases the possibility of the "great star" being a blazing object from an origin different from the actual heaven.

Let us now examine what the verb, "fell," in Revelation 8:10 means. Its original Greek term, ἔπεσεν (*epesen*), is a second aorist form of πίπτω (*piptō*; to fall). One of the meanings of the verb πίπτω (*piptō*; to fall) is "to fall down," as in descending "from an erect to a prostrate position."[25] One example is as follows:

> [Mt 2:11] And when they were come into the house, they saw the young child with Mary his mother, and *fell down* (πίπτω, *piptō*), and worshipped him: and when they had opened their treasures, they presented unto him gifts; gold, and frankincense, and myrrh.

As in the way the verb πίπτω (*piptō*; to fall down) is used in Matthew 2:11, the expression in Revelation 8:10 may also be translated to mean: a star descended from heights as if prostrating toward (or drooping over) the land. Keeping this in mind, let us re-read the passage:

> [Rev 8:10] And the third angel sounded, and there fell a great star from heaven, burning as it were a lamp, and it *fell* upon the third part of the rivers, and upon the fountains of waters;

What is worth noting here is that a star (singular) fell over a wide area of regions as if a lump was pulverized into infinitesimal pieces before they were dispersed and drooped over the rivers. Indeed, the lump of the radioactive particles of Chernobyl shot up to the sky like a burning lamp, and the particles were carried by wind to broad areas, and then fell down to the fountains of waters by rain.

So far, historical accounts of the Chernobyl nuclear incident matched exactly with the interpretation on the third trumpet. However, there are other interpretational attempts on the third trumpet. Focusing on the fact that it is called a "star," some theorized the third trumpet to be some sort of an asteroid and/or comet impact. Their main point is that a chemical change by the asteroid or comet entering the atmosphere causes the oxygen and nitrogen to produce nitric acid rain.[26]

However, as discussed before, the nitric acid rain can be effectively filtered out by water purifiers. Not only the filtration can remedy the problem, but also, there has been no such incident that particularly matches with the name Wormwood or Chernobyl that God has provided. Indeed, when a name such as Wormwood is specified, God may be suggesting where the event occurs or originates from.

Some even advocate naming a future meteor or comet Wormwood, should it collide with the earth, but deliberately naming a future object in effort to fulfill God's prophecy is certainly going overboard.

Even if such meteoric collision occurs, the chance of people dying from drinking the water will almost be non-existent. Supposing that contaminants from an asteroid or a comet got mixed in the water, today's filter technology would be able to remove such contaminants to produce potable water, as already discussed.

The only exception to filterable contaminants would be of radioactive nature. Therefore, when the Scripture recorded water turning bitter, it may have been referring to a more fundamental chemical change than a mere mixing of compounds or molecules with water. In conclusion, neither asteroid nor comet theory can fully satisfy Wormwood prophecy; only the Chernobyl Nuclear

Power Plant disaster in 1986 uniquely befits the descriptions of the third trumpet and confirms Scriptural interpretation.

CHAPTER 4.
THE SECOND TRUMPET:
A GREAT MOUNTAIN
BURNING WITH FIRE

If the third trumpet occurred in 1986, the second trumpet must have been sounded prior to that year. The Scripture pertaining to the second trumpet appears in Revelation chapter 8:

[Rev 8:8] And the second angel sounded, and as it were a great mountain burning with fire was cast into *the* sea: and *the* third part of *the* sea became blood;
[Rev 8:9] And *the* third part of *the* creatures which were in *the* sea, and had life, died; and *the* third part of *the* ships were destroyed.

World War II: The Atomic Bombing of Hiroshima

The historical incident that satisfies all the prophetic descriptions in this passage happened during World War II (1939–1945) that involved over 100 countries. Except for some neutral states, almost all countries participated in World War II.

The fatalities due to WWII are estimated to be about 66 million.[1] WWII came to a sudden stop when atomic bombs were dropped on Hiroshima and Nagasaki of Japan in 1945.

Revelation 8:8 writes that something like a great mountain burning with fire was cast into the sea. That very sea represents Japan, an island country in the middle of the sea! Something like a great mountain burning with fire corresponds to the mushroom cloud from the atomic bombing. As a result of detonation, the third part of the area became blood.

What is noticeable in Revelation 8:8–9 is that the definite article "the" appears several times in this passage. The presence of definite article plays important role in interpreting this Scripture, as in the following examples.

In verse 8, something like "a great mountain burning with fire" is cast into "the sea." This sea is not the whole sea of the earth but a specific region denoted by the definite article "the." Therefore, "the sea" specifically refers to a location where the detonation occurred.

Likewise, in calculating "the third part of the creatures which were in the sea" mentioned in verse 9, the fatalities specifically in the detonated region should be investigated.

The first step to the investigation is finding out what it means by "creatures." This is best done by referring to the usage of the word in the Bible. The following verses use the same word "creatures."

> [Jas 1:18] Of his own will begat he us with the word of truth, that we should be a kind of firstfruits of his *creatures*.
>
> [Rev 5:13] And every *creature* which is in heaven, and on the earth, and under the earth, and such as are in the sea, and all that are in them, heard I saying, Blessing, and honour, and glory, and power, be unto him that sitteth upon the throne, and unto the Lamb for ever and ever.

The verses above indicate that the "creatures" include mankind. Thus, the fatalities in the detonated city can confirm the fulfillment of the prophecy of the second trumpet.

Between Hiroshima and Nagasaki, which city should be investigated for fatalities? An atomic bomb was dropped on each of the two cities then, but the Scripture only records prophecy on one city. This can be deduced from the phrase, "a great mountain burning with fire" in verse 8, which is singular, not plural. Then which city did John see in his vision? The answer can be derived from examining the death toll from both cities.

Let us first examine the death toll in the city of Hiroshima. The population of Hiroshima then ranged from 340,000 to 350,000, and the fatalities due to the atomic detonation are estimated to be around 90,000 to 166,000. The estimated fatality rate is between 25.7 percent and 48.8 percent of the population then.

In the case of Nagasaki, its population then ranged from 250,000 to 270,000, out of which 60,000 to 80,000 died from the atomic bomb. The estimated fatality rate in Nagasaki therefore is between 22.2 percent and 32.0 percent of the population.[2]

Revelation 8:9 says that "the third part of the creatures which were in the sea, and had life, died." Comparing the statistics does not provide an absolute indicator as to which city was detonated in John's vision. Nonetheless, taking into account that the maximum fatality rate in Nagasaki reaches 32 percent, a bit less than the third, it can be argued that it is more probable that John saw the atomic bombing in the city of Hiroshima. The numbers in the *Truman Papers* also support this argument, as it reported that 30 percent of Hiroshima population died from the blast and another 30 percent severely injured.[3]

If there is another reason to believe what John saw in his vision was the bombing of Hiroshima, it is the date of the bombing. Hiroshima was the target of the first nuclear bombing mission on August 6, whereas Nagasaki was an alternative secondary target scheduled for later dates and bombed on August 9. Therefore, it is more likely that God showed John the first-ever weapon of mass destruction in application. As seen throughout the interpretations of the seals and the trumpets, God consistently showed a series of historical incidents, each of which was the first or significant incident of its kind that sets the precedent in history for coming generations. In like manner, the world's first atomic bomb on the Japanese city of Hiroshima is likely what John witnessed in his vision.

Revelation 8:9 also states that "the third part of the ships were destroyed." Toward the end of World War II, high-speed bombers and jets had been developed and the role of air forces became prominent. Following WWII, world powers focused on fortifying their aircrafts. But at the dawn of WWII, warfare was still marked as the battle of naval forces. As Revelation 8:9 says "the third part of the ships were destroyed," investigation on the number of the ships involved in the war is needed.

Much investigation on this topic has been done by Irvin Baxter, who provided the number of total ships that participated in WWII—105,127 ships—for transporting humans, food, artillery, fuel, and others, and the total number of ships that sunk during WWII—36,387 ships. Calculation revealed that nearly one-third (34.6 percent) of all the ships sunk during WWII, which is exactly what the Bible predicted.[4] Therefore, Revelation 8:9 was fulfilled just as it was written.

Some may question: why does confirming the death of the third part of the creatures include the population from Hiroshima only, while the calculation of the third part of the ships destroyed includes the entire number of ships utilized for war mobilization?

The answer to this is rather simple. As for "*the* third part of *the* creatures," they are limited to those "which were in *the* sea," as specified in Revelation 8:9, while for "*the* third part of *the* ships," they are not confined to "*the* sea." In other words, the number of ships must be all-inclusive of those mobilized for the entire WWII warfare. In calculating those that were destroyed and confirming that the third of the ships were destroyed, the total number of the ships of Japan and other nations as well should be taken into account.

A Bomb Detonated First, then Cast

Finally, can the Hiroshima atomic bombing be described as something "burning with fire" that was "cast into the sea" after having been set on fire, as described in Revelation 8:8? Normally, bombs detonate upon coming into contact with its target object. Only then the object catches fire with an explosion. If this was the case, should not the description be reversed in order and be, "as it were a great mountain was cast into the sea and burned with fire"? To answer this question, let us scrutinize the Scripture:

> [Rev 8:8] And the second angel sounded, and as it were a great mountain burning with fire was cast *into the sea* (εἰς τὴν θάλασσαν, *eis tēn thalassan*): and the third part of the sea became blood;

The expression "into the sea" (εἰς τὴν θάλασσαν, *eis tēn thalassan*) has a preposition εἰς (*eis*) which means: "into, unto, to, towards, for, among."[5] To understand the significance of this expression, the atomic bomb used on Hiroshima needs to be examined and understood.

The atomic bomb dropped on Hiroshima, Japan was named "Little Boy." Regarding this bomb, the National Science Digital Library provides the following explanation: "On August 6, 1945, it was exploded at an altitude of about 1,900 feet (600 m) above the city of Hiroshima, Japan."[6] This statement testifies that the nuclear weapons are unlike conventional bombs in that they explode in the sky before destroying anything on ground-level. In actuality, the atomic bomb was dropped to first create the mountain-like burning explosion (see Fig. 4-2) and then cast unto, to, or towards the target site in Japan. This is just as the Bible has prophesied the second trumpet, with descriptions and word choices alarmingly accurate.

Fig. 4-1. A mock-up of the "Little Boy" nuclear weapon dropped on Hiroshima, Japan, in August 1945. Photo courtesy of US National Archives and Records Administration.

Fig. 4-2. The mushroom cloud over Hiroshima after the dropping of "Little Boy." Photo courtesy of US Army.

CHAPTER 5.
THE FIRST TRUMPET:
HAIL AND FIRE MINGLED WITH
BLOOD

Like the second trumpet, the Scripture pertaining to the first trumpet appears in Revelation chapter 8 as well:

> [Rev 8:6] And the seven angels which had the seven trumpets prepared themselves to sound.
> [Rev 8:7] The first angel sounded, and there followed hail and fire mingled with blood, and they were cast upon *the* earth: and *the* third part of trees was burnt up, and all green grass was burnt up.

The second trumpet, World War II, occurred from 1939 to 1945. Thus, the first trumpet must have been sounded before the year 1939. What historical incident could the passage above be referring to? What significant incident happened before WWII that involved casualties of humans and environment? Review of history revealed that this incident was World War I.

World War I: A Trench Warfare

World War I erupted in 1914 and the total fatalities are estimated to be 15 million.[1] WWI is famous for its trench warfare. To protect the army from the enemy's small-arms and artillery fire, the warfare involved much digging of trenches, especially at the Western Front.[2]

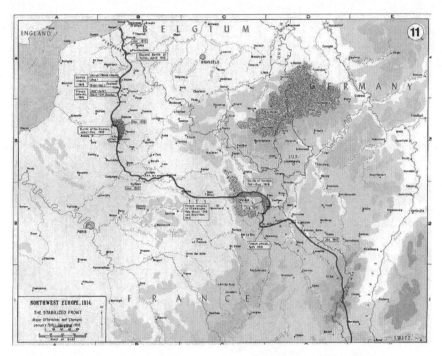

Fig. 5-1. Map of the Western Front, 1915–1916. The bold line on the map shows where the trenches stretched from the North Sea to the Swiss border. Photo courtesy of US Military Academy.

In Fig. 5-1, the bold line indicates where the fiercest trench warfare took place, including the city in France, Somme. The battle of Somme is the bloodiest battle of WWI on the Western Front. British casualties were known to be over 400,000.[3]

This trench warfare continued until the end of 1918, when the Armistice of Villa Giusti finally called for the suspension of hostility between Italy and Austria-Hungary on the Italian Front.

By November 11th of that year, what became later known as the Armistice Day finally came.

WWI brought many new changes to how wars were fought. The artillery underwent the most revolutionary and scientific advances during WWI. Trenches were developed into underground bunkers. Poison gas was used for the first time.[4] Bayonets, pistols, rifles, machine guns, flamethrowers, grenades, and tanks were also used.[5] Some lighter-weight weaponry such as trench mortar was also developed, designed to fire a projectile at a steep angle, usually more than 45 degrees, so that it can reach enemies in the trench by falling down straightly.[6]

The heavy explosives bombarded everything in the terrain in between the two opposing armies' trenches. The destruction was so devastating that the terrain was later given the term "No Man's Land" (see Fig. 5-2). The intensive bombardment reshaped the terrain by not only burning up many green trees in the war zones, but also burning up all the green grass and overturning soil to the extent that the Earth's surface crust was destroyed in the area, exposing the next soil layer underneath. This "No Man's Land" is most probably "the earth" that had the third part of trees burnt up and all green grass burnt up, as Revelation 8:7 records.

Fig. 5-2. The badly shelled main road to Bapaume, France. Photo by User: Hohum via Wikimedia Commons.

An excerpt from frontiernet.net on Marne, France, where one of the most notorious battles at the Western Front was fought, reads:

> Wooded areas were destroyed utterly and the topsoil was blasted away to the unyielding, underlying chalk . . . forty-three bombs per minute, over thirty-six thousand in fourteen hours, fell on the city . . . The combination of shelling, entrenchments, and mining removed soil to underlying chalk in the most devastated regions and without a layer of topsoil the earth cannot support agriculture.[7]

Enormous amount of heavy artillery use during WWI devastated agriculture and vegetation in the war zones. The "No Man's Land" was literally a no-green-tree-nor-grass-land as pictured in Fig. 5-2.

Hail and Fire Mingled with Blood?

One might ask: if "hail" describes falling of the artillery shells, is it not strange that "hail and fire mingled with blood"?

> [Rev 8:7] The first angel sounded, and there followed *hail and fire mingled with blood,* and they were cast upon the earth: and the third part of trees was burnt up, and all green grass was burnt up.

In general, shells are not prepared by mixing with blood. Rather, they cause bloodshed after getting detonated on the ground. Then why did the KJV translate as if hail and fire mixed with blood before hitting the ground?

The verb "mingle" is μίγνυμι (*mignumi*) in Greek which is often used with different prepositions. Two verses using one of the prepositions are as follows:

[Mt 27:34] They gave him vinegar to drink *mingled with gall:* and when he had tasted thereof, he would not drink.

[Lk 13:1] There were present at that season some that told him of the Galilaeans, whose blood Pilate had *mingled with their sacrifices.*

In both cases, the preposition μετά (*meta;* with) is used with the verb "mingle." However, in Revelation 8:7, it is used together with ἐν (*en;* in).

Regarding the dissimilar use of the word "mingle" in combination with preposition ἐν (*en;* in), *Vincent's Word Studies* commented:

> *Hail and fire mingled with blood* (χάλαζα καὶ πῦρ μεμιγμένα αἵματι). Insert ἐν *in* before αἵματι *blood.* Instead of *"with* blood" as A.V., and Rev., we should render *"in* blood." The hailstones and fire-balls fell in a shower of blood.[8]

In conclusion, the Scripture is not describing the hail mixed with blood, but instead the hail (bomb shells) mingling into the blood of dying men. The verse in question accurately describes the high-angle artillery projectile war of WWI, where the shells were falling almost vertically from the sky like a hail.

Up to this point, the volume covered the first, second, and third trumpets. These interpretations match the works of some other scholars.[9, 10] By interpreting the events nevertheless, it was the authors' wish to elaborate on the accuracy of the Scripture in its descriptions and word choices, and to confirm historical facts in the process. In interpreting the rest of the trumpets in the book of Revelation, a profound approach was taken in analyzing and probing the history.

CHAPTER 6.
THE FOURTH TRUMPET:
THE THIRD PART OF THE SUN, THE
MOON, AND THE STARS SMITTEN

The third trumpet was interpreted to have occurred in 1986. The fourth trumpet then would have occurred after 1986. The passage on the fourth trumpet is as follows:

> [Rev 8:12] And the fourth angel sounded, and *the third part of the sun was smitten*, and the third part of the moon, and the third part of the stars; so as the third part of them was darkened, and the day shone not for a third part of it, and the night likewise.

What does it mean by the third part of the sun, the moon and the stars being smitten to darkness? This most likely does not mean that the celestial bodies will actually dim in brightness, but that there is some kind of screening effects due to air particulates such as smoke. Similar examples appear in other places in the Bible:

> [Rev 9:2] And he opened the bottomless pit; and there arose a smoke out of the pit, as the smoke of a great furnace; and *the sun and the air were darkened by reason of the smoke* of the pit.

[Eze 32:7] And when I shall put thee out, I will cover the heaven, and make the stars thereof dark; I will *cover the sun with a cloud, and the moon shall not give her light.*

In these verses also the sun was darkened. But clearly, they are not referring to the phenomenon of the actual sun becoming dark. The real reason for the darkening is provided: the covering by smoke and cloud. In Revelation chapter 8 also, it would be more plausible to interpret that the sun, the moon and the stars were altogether darkened by some smoke's screening effect rather than to say that celestial bodies dimmed in reality.

Besides, what would be the probability that all the sun, the moon, and the stars become dark at the same time? It would be very unlikely. Therefore, it is plausible to reason that the dimming of the celestial bodies is a result of changes in the Earth's atmosphere.

Chemtrails

As established previously, since the third trumpet was sounded in 1986, the fourth trumpet must have been sounded sometime after 1986. A very well-documented video from the Discovery Channel on the topic of chemical contrail called *chemtrail* provides insights into a possible interpretation on the fourth trumpet as chemtrail and reveals the use of chemtrail dating back to as early as 1990.[1]

It is presumed that the spraying of chemtrail in the sky started with the intent to reduce the global warming through geoengineering. Fine aerosols of metallic origins like aluminum oxide introduced in the atmosphere would reflect the sunlight back into the space outside Earth. It is reported that the chemtrail contains "unusual high spikes in chemicals and heavy metals [such as] barium, aluminum, manganese, magnesium, zinc."[2]

Nowadays, it is common to see military airplanes diligently releasing chemicals into the atmosphere, and more than often, a white haze or a giant checkerboard remains in the sky instead of the deep blue sky. The white lines of these chemtrails would not fade away even for hours at times.

Normal contrails consisting of water vapors would fade away in seconds to minutes usually. Fig. 6-1 is what the National Oceanic and Atmospheric Administration (NOAA) claims to be contrails,[3] but many contend that they are chemtrails.

Fig. 6-1. Multiple persistent contrails. Photo courtesy of US NOAA.

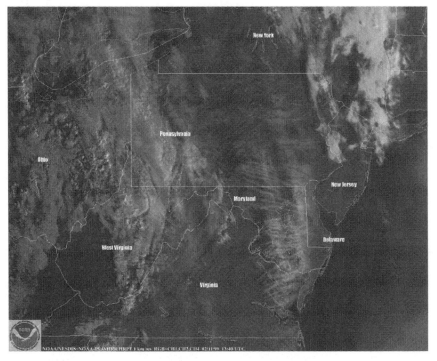

Fig. 6-2. NOAA image taken on September 22, 2000.
Photo courtesy of US NOAA.

Fig. 6-2 is an aerial photo shot over the East Coast of the United States taken in the year 2000. The white hazy lines present over Maryland and Pennsylvania are very conspicuously man-made.

Fig. 6-3. Enhanced infrared image taken on January 29, 2004. Photo courtesy of NASA.

Fig. 6-3 is also an aerial shot of the southeastern part of the United States. Underneath the white streaks and hazy lines, the landscape of Florida, Alabama, Georgia, and South Carolina is barely visible in some areas. NASA claims that these are "contrail clutter," but they remain in the sky without dissipating for hours. Thus, their true identity is debated, whether they are contrail or chemtrail.[4]

Fig. 6-4. NOAA image of Saudi Arabia, taken on Jan.
28, 1991. Photo courtesy of US NOAA.

Fig. 6-4 is another photo, an aerial view over Saudi Arabia
taken in 1991 by NOAA. As the Discovery Channel documentary
revealed, the chemtrails were used in Vietnam War for the
purpose of engineering the weather in the region.[5]

It is suspected that the chemtrail spraying became an international standard routine starting in the early 1990s for the express purpose of slowing down the global warming through geoengineering. Needless to say, these chemtrails have a direct impact on reducing the light of the sun, the moon and the stars entering Earth during day time as well as night time.

To see how the chemtrail is used with specific purpose, let us review some of the legal documents of the past. The House Resolution 2977, the Space Preservation Act of 2001,[6] under the Section 7 Definitions, reads:

> (II) through the use of land-based, sea-based, or space-based systems using radiation, electromagnetic, psychotronic, sonic, laser, or other energies directed at individual persons or targeted populations for the purpose of information war, mood management, or mind control of such persons or populations; or
> (III) by expelling chemical or biological agents in the vicinity of a person.
>
> (B) Such terms include exotic weapons systems such as—
>
> (i) electronic, psychotronic, or information weapons;
> (ii) *chemtrails;*
> (iii) high altitude ultra low frequency weapons systems;
> (iv) plasma, electromagnetic, sonic, or ultrasonic weapons;
> (v) laser weapons systems;
> (vi) strategic, theater, tactical, or extraterrestrial weapons; and
> (vii) chemical, biological, environmental, climate, or tectonic weapons.

From this Act, it is evident that the politicians and some law makers are fully aware of the existence and the potential uses of the chemtrails and other various weapons.

The last paragraph of the HR 2977 reads:

> (C) The term "exotic weapons systems" includes weapons designed to damage space or natural ecosystems (such as the ionosphere and upper atmosphere) or climate, weather, and tectonic systems with the purpose of inducing damage or destruction upon a target population or region on earth or in space.[7]

The exotic weapons to control climate, weather and even the people's minds are not a science fiction anymore. They exist and are covertly implemented in reality.

The HR 2977 was actually introduced to put a stop on the research, development, testing, manufacturing, production, and deployment of all exotic weapons. However, with "unfavorable executive comment received from the Department of Defense," the HR 2977 was not passed into law.[8]

Later, HR 3657 (108th): Space Preservation Act of 2003[9] and HR 2420 of 2005[10] were referred to the House subcommittee, but the detailed listing of exotic weapons under definition section was reduced to projectiles and explosives, and excluded chemtrails.

The US Department of Defense is involved with the use of "chaff," which is made from various fibrous and metallic material, and "works like a decoy by presenting a false target to enemy radar systems."[11]

The report from the General Accounting Office (GAO) in 1998 regarding the *Department of Defense Management Issues Related to Chaff* reveals certain objectives the chaff serves, releasing detailed information such as the types and inventories of the chaffs used by the Air Force, the Navy and the Army.[12]

The report continues to say:

> It has been used by the military for more than 50 years. It was used during World War II and more recently during Operation Desert Storm . . . The first recorded large-scale use of chaff by American forces in combat was on December 20, 1943, in an air raid by 8th Air Force bombers over Bremen, Germany. Today, the services use chaff on combat ranges and at other locations worldwide for peacetime training and testing.[13]

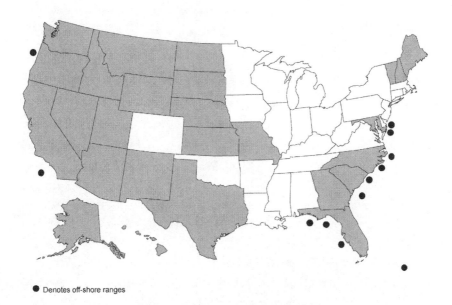

● Denotes off-shore ranges

Fig. 6-5. States (shaded) and off-shore ranges where chaff is used. Photo courtesy of US GAO.

Attached in the report is the radar image of chaff plumes over Arizona and New Mexico region in 1997 (Fig. 6-6). Such a self-explanatory image is indicative of potential applications of these chaffs at different density levels.

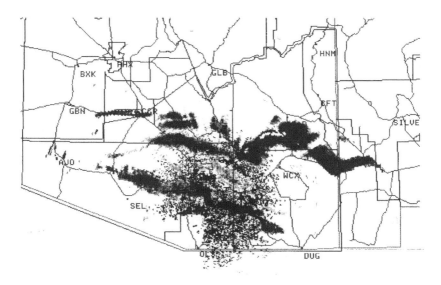

Fig. 6-6. Radar image of chaff plumes over Arizona and New Mexico in 1997. Photo courtesy of US GAO.

The *Idaho Observer* in 2006 disclosed that the chemtrail is what the GAO report admits as "chaff". It further revealed that the substances found in the chaff sprayed over Iowa included: "6 bacteria including anthrax and pneumonia; 9 chemicals including acetylcholine chloride; 26 heavy metals including arsenic, gold, lead, mercury, silver, uranium, and zinc; 4 molds and fungi; 7 viruses; 2 cancers; 2 vaccines; and 2 sedatives."[14]

The GAO report raises concern against the unintended effects the chaffs bring on the environment. The chaff sends false radar images that are misinterpreted as rainy clouds and cause confusion in weather forecast, thereby interfering with the launching of space shuttles.[15] Despite technical advantages for military purposes, the environmental issues arising from its use seem very serious, according to the GAO report.

Global Dimming

In addition to the chemtrail, climatological phenomena studied by many researchers in the academia substantiate the fulfillment of Revelation's fourth trumpet prophecy.

A study published in the *International Journal of Climatology* in 1997 investigated recent changes in the solar radiation at two sites in Germany. It concluded that the "global solar radiation for overcast conditions . . . decreased by an average rate of 8% per decade between 1964 and 1990,"[16] which accounts for over 20 percent reduction in the solar radiation for overcast conditions during the period. But as this decrease was observed only during overcast conditions, it is not comprehensively representative of the changes of the entire global solar radiation. For this reported change to be interpreted as the fourth trumpet, the solar radiation levels during clear and cloudy conditions needed to be observed also.

Nevertheless, it is important to note from the study's conclusion that "possible reasons" for the reduced solar radiation are partly due to "the aircraft traffic increasing the occurrence of cirrus clouds and an indirect aerosol effect."[17] In essence, this study is supportive of the fact that the contrail and chemtrail contribute to Global Dimming in the Earth's atmosphere. In fact, reports have been made that the contrail effect on the solar radiation reduction is greater than previously thought.[18]

Fig. 6-7 from another study shows that the global solar radiation was reduced at all eight stations in Germany except Braunschweig over 27 years period up until 1990. For all sky conditions, "the average decline of the daily means is 10 W m^{-2} (= 4%) per decade and is statistically significant for five out of the eight stations." The researchers further make an interesting

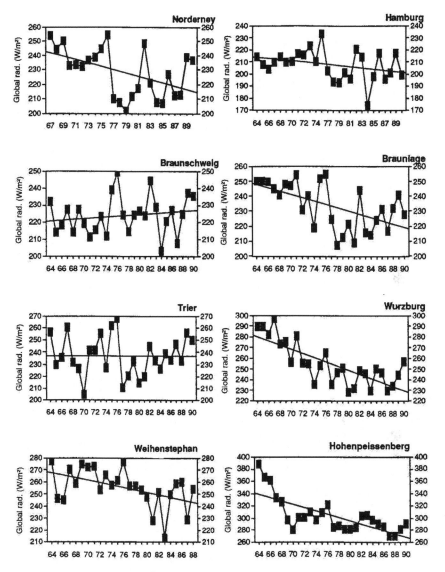

Fig. 6-7. Time series and trends of the annual global solar radiation at surface at eight German stations from 1964 to 1990. © American Meteorological Society. Used with permission.

conclusion: "Although the present study is limited to only a few German stations each affected by local conditions, we believe that the results are reasonably representative of rural, industrial, as well as urban environments of Western and Central Europe."[19]

A similar study conducted in China arrived at similar conclusions. The study published in *Geophysical Research Letters* in 2008 reveals the long-term trends in sunshine duration over two provinces in China.[20]

In summary, "Yunnan-Guizhou Plateau (YGP), a low latitude highland region, covers the two provinces of Yunnan and Guizhou in Southwest China, where a cooling trend in the annual mean surface air temperature since the mid-20th century was reported as a notable phenomenon of regional climate against the global warming."[21]

The researchers "applied the data of sunshine duration and cloud amount from 184 stations across the YGP from year 1961 to 2005" and found "that, over this 45 year period, annual sunshine duration decreased mostly north of 24°N on the YGP . . . −11.8% per decade," and "an overall decline in annual sunshine duration over the northern YGP dramatically accelerated from the 1970s to 80s with its maximum rate in the 1980s." But just as in the study in Germany, the "annual mean cloud amount . . . was shown to be insignificant and even in decline over the 45 years," so they reached the same conclusion "support[ing] the hypothesis that aerosol loading in the atmosphere could be involved in the surface cooling trend."[22]

A paper from Japan, published in *International Journal of Climatology* in 2003, arrives at the same conclusion. The summary points taken from the "discussion and conclusions" section of the paper state:

The sunshine from spring to autumn in northern Japan has obviously decreased in the late 1980s and the 1990s, and the period of little sunshine has become longer since the mid-1980s. In CW [central and western] Japan, a period of relatively little sunshine often appeared in late spring during the 1950s and the early 1960s . . . In the Southwest Islands, sunshine duration has been decreasing almost all through the year; as a result, . . . a temporal fine-weather period around April has disappeared . . . What are the physical mechanisms of the climatic variations that explain the secular change of seasonal transitions of sunshine duration revealed in the present study? The time and spatial scales of these variations are relatively large; thus, local-scale air pollution does not seem to be the main reason. It seems that decadal-scale modulations of the seasonal cycle of atmospheric circulation patterns exist in East Asia, and the causes may be natural climatic variations and/or long-term anthropogenic climate changes, such as global warming.[23]

Such observations steadily occurred from 1950s since systematic measurement on the solar radiation started. On average, it was reported that, from the late 1950s to the early 1990s, the solar radiation declined as much as 5 percent worldwide.[24]

The decline varied depending on the sites: in Antarctica, the solar radiation to the earth's surface dropped 9 percent, and in the United States, it was reduced by 10 percent during the period. In parts of the British Isles, 16 percent decrease was observed, while in Israel, about 22 percent was observed. In Russia, there was an almost 30 percent drop, and in Hong Kong, the sunlight decreased by 37 percent![25, 26, 27]

In other words, some parts of the globe, Russia and Hong Kong, for example, had already reached the one-third reduction of the solar radiation sufficiently by the early 1990s.

Dr. Beate G. Liepert, a climatologist, explains the possible causes of the solar radiation reduction or Global Dimming:

> What is going on? In a word, pollution . . . Pollution dims sunlight in two ways. First, it bounces incoming light off the airborne particles and back into space. Second, the pollution causes more water droplets to condense out of the air, leading to darker, thicker clouds—which, of course, block more sunlight. Global warming also contributes to dimming: warmer air holds more water, and when condensed the warmer clouds are heavier and darker. For that reason, the dimming appears to be more pronounced on cloudy days than sunny ones.[28]

As the developed nations had been trying hard to reduce the air pollution, the rate of the solar radiation reduction has decreased or stopped during the 1990s. Actually, "satellites measured less global cloud coverage from the early 1990s to 2002."[29]

In the northern YGP region of China, the decline in the sunshine duration has "remarkably decelerated since the 1990s so that going into the twenty-first century the annual sunshine duration has ceased or even reversed its downward tendency."[30] Note that here, "deceleration" means that the rate of the solar radiation reduction is decreasing. Although the rate was decreasing in the 1990s, the solar radiation reduction was still progressing as far as the rate is non-negative. It can be said that the greatest reduction in the solar radiation in YGP region of China reached around the year 2000 when the rate reversed into a negative value.

A BBC documentary in 2005 states:

> In Western Europe the steps we have taken to cut air pollution have started to bear fruit in a noticeable improvement in air quality and even a slight reduction in Global Dimming over the last few years. Yet at the same time, after decades in which they held steady, European temperatures have started rapidly to rise culminating in the savage summer of 2003.[31]

It is not possible to pinpoint when the fourth trumpet was sounded — when the third part of the sun, the moon, and the stars was smitten and was darkened so that "the day shone not for a third part of it, and the night likewise." Yet the discussions above indicate that the reduction of the solar radiation by 30 percent certainly happened by or after the 1990s in certain regions. The reduction continued through, while the rate started to decrease or stop throughout the 1990s.

It is safe to say that, perhaps the culmination of Global Dimming happened around the year 2000 as "a slight reduction in Global Dimming [was observed] over the last few years [of 2005]."[32]

The third trumpet, the Chernobyl Nuclear Plant explosion, was sounded in 1986, and the fourth trumpet is a post-third trumpet event. Global Dimming, due to chemtrails and other reasons, culminating around the year 2000 corresponds to the fourth trumpet event, nicely fitting the timeline provided in Revelation.

In sum, although the sun itself was as bright as before, the solar radiation reaching the surface of Earth has decreased substantially. This was a global phenomenon, termed as "Global Dimming." As said, some parts of Earth had already reached the state of 30 percent reduction in the solar radiation in the early 1990s. The prophecy that "the third part of the sun was smitten" was accomplished, along with the moon and the stars. Therefore, the science community validates that Global Dimming, the fourth trumpet, had already been sounded at the turn of millennium.

The Gulf War?

There are some people who interpret that the Gulf War is the fourth trumpet. But simple facts suggest this theory is unlikely. The Persian Gulf War started on August 2, 1990 and continued until February 28, 1991. On January 23rd, Saddam Hussein ordered the dumping of 400 million gallons of crude oil into the Persian Gulf, as a deliberate means to keep US Marine forces from coming ashore. This caused the largest offshore oil spill in history at that time.[33]

Before retreating from Kuwait in February 1991, Iraqi troops had set about 700 oil wells on fire to prevent the US from taking advantage of the oil fields.[34] One can imagine how much black smoke arose from the fire. The footage from the war shows a lot of smoke rising in the region. It is probable to speculate that the sun, the moon and the stars were hidden from the smoke at that time. For these reasons, there are people who interpret the Persian Gulf War to be the fourth trumpet.

Yet, the Gulf War was a localized incident in Kuwait only, not an incident that occurred on a grand scale, as opposed to all the seal and the trumpet events that have been interpreted. As established in Volume 1, the historical incidents corresponding to the seals were significant milestones in history, with their artifacts and cultural remains continuing for a long time, often to this date.

The first trumpet was interpreted to be World War I. The second trumpet, World War II. The third trumpet, the Chernobyl Nuclear Plant explosion. These trumpet incidents were also significant milestones in history; incidents of grand scale that affected a significant portion of world population and/or the globe. The fourth trumpet? It is probably more likely that this incident also affected Earth and its inhabitants on a similar scale, as Global Dimming did. In other words, the chance of Gulf War being an appropriate interpretation for the fourth trumpet is slim.

With all that said, there are two events that can be interpreted as the fourth trumpet: firstly, the chemtrails, and secondly, Global Dimming from the reduction of solar and other celestial radiation caused by natural and/or anthropogenic climate changes. But if only one incident should be selected to explain the prophecy, the qualifier would be Global Dimming, since the chemtrail may be one of many factors that cause Global Dimming. The chemtrail alone may not be sufficient to cause Global Dimming, and Global Dimming may have multiple factors contributing to its phenomenon. In this sense, the fourth trumpet may be labeled as Global Dimming culminating around the year 2000, and its interpretation seems to line up well as a post-1986 incident, an incident after the Chernobyl disaster.

Relating the chemtrails to interpreting the fourth trumpet had already been proclaimed on the authors' YouTube channel in 2011, and Global Dimming likewise in 2013 on YouTube by the authors. In this regard, the authors may be one of the first to interpret the fourth trumpet as the Global Dimming phenomenon.

CHAPTER 7.
THE FIFTH TRUMPET:
A SMOKE OUT OF THE BOTTOMLESS PIT

The fourth trumpet has been interpreted as Global Dimming culminating circa 2000. Therefore, the fifth trumpet must be a post-2000 incident, which brings it closer to the current time. Should the fifth trumpet have already been sounded, it really deserves full attention, for the day of the Lord's return is even closer according to the apocalyptic timeline.

Features of the Fifth Trumpet

With that said, let us study about the fifth trumpet by reading the passage, which takes up a big portion of Revelations chapter 9, from verses 1 to 12:

> [Rev 9:1] And the fifth angel sounded, and I saw a star fall from heaven unto the earth: and to him was given the key of the bottomless pit.
> [Rev 9:2] And he opened the bottomless pit; and there arose a *smoke out of the pit*, as the smoke of a great furnace; and the sun and the air were darkened by reason of the smoke of the pit.

[Rev 9:3] And there came out of the smoke *locusts* upon the earth: and unto them was given power, as the scorpions of the earth have power.

[Rev 9:4] And it was commanded them that they should not hurt the grass of the earth, neither any green thing, neither any tree; but only those men which have not the seal of God in their foreheads.

[Rev 9:5] And to them it was given that they should *not kill* them, but that they should be *tormented five months*: and their torment was as the torment of a scorpion, when he striketh a man.

[Rev 9:6] And in those days shall [the] men seek death, and shall not find it; and shall desire to die, and death shall flee from them.

According to the passage, there must be a smoke rising out of the bottomless pit and locusts coming out of the smoke during the fifth trumpet event. The people who do not have the seal of God in their foreheads must suffer from the tormenting activity, but not be killed. Only the incident that meets all these requirements can fulfill the prophecy. The passage continues in verse 7:

[Rev 9:7] And the shapes of the locusts were like unto horses prepared unto battle; and on their heads were as it were crowns like gold, and their faces were as the faces of men.

[Rev 9:8] And they had hair as the hair of women, and their teeth were as the teeth of lions.

[Rev 9:9] And they had breastplates, as it were breastplates of iron; and the sound of their wings was as the sound of chariots of many horses running to battle.

[Rev 9:10] And they had tails like unto scorpions, and there were stings in their tails: and their power was to hurt [the] men five months.

[Rev 9:11] And they had a king over them, which is the angel of the bottomless pit, whose name in the Hebrew tongue is Abaddon, but in the Greek tongue hath his name Apollyon.

[Rev 9:12] One woe is past; and, behold, there come two woes more hereafter.

The description of the fifth trumpet ends here. There are several features that constitute this prophecy:

a) Smoke arises out of the pit.

b) There is a presence of locusts.

c) The locusts should not hurt the grass of the earth, neither any green thing, neither any tree.

d) The locusts torment men, but no one dies.

e) The locusts have power to torment men for five months.

f) The locusts have a king, whose name is Abaddon/Apollyon. The meaning of the name Abaddon/Apollyon is "destroyer."[1]

If any of the aforesaid conditions does not satisfy, the incident cannot be considered as the fifth trumpet. Any incident interpreted with incorrect premise cannot be the corresponding candidate for the prophetic event, however logically intricate or closely resembling it may sound.

The Gulf War?

The Persian Gulf War of 1990 to 1991 was briefly reviewed in the previous chapter, in discussion of the fourth trumpet. Iraq's leader then was Saddam Hussein, and the name *Saddam* means "destroyer," the meaning of Abaddon or Apollyon. Therefore, some interpret the Gulf War as the fifth trumpet, not only because of the name Abaddon/Apollyon but also because this leader fought against a coalition of thirty-four countries and used helicopters, airborne forces that look like locusts, to fight over Kuwait City.[2]

Yet, this interpretation is not free of problems, as Saddam Hussein was later captured and executed in 2006. While some may insist that Saddam actually did not die and still remains alive, the fact is that Saddam Hussein died. The problem ensues from a conventional perspective that the name *Abaddon* is the name of the Antichrist.[3] According to the Bible, Jesus Christ will capture the Antichrist at the time of His return. The basis for this conventional argument can be found in the following verses:

> [Rev 17:8] The *beast* that thou sawest was, and is not; and shall ascend out of the *bottomless pit*, and go into perdition: and they that dwell on the earth shall wonder, whose names were not written in the book of life from the foundation of the world, when they behold the *beast* that was, and is not, and yet is.
> [Rev 19:20] And the *beast* was taken, and with him the false prophet that wrought miracles before him, with which he deceived them that had received the mark of the *beast*, and them that worshipped his image. These both were cast alive into a lake of fire burning with brimstone.

According to the Scripture, both the beast and the false prophet who worked miracles will be caught and cast alive into a lake of fire by Lord Jesus. The argument that Abaddon/Apollyon in Revelation 9 is the beast in Revelation 17 is based on the fact that these two figures are related to the bottomless pit.

Thus, the problem becomes obvious. If Abaddon is the name of the beast who is also the Antichrist, then it is Abaddon that Jesus Himself will capture to finish him. If Saddam who represents Abaddon died already, then an apparent contradiction arises. Even if Saddam's name means "destroyer" and may be equivalent to Abaddon/Apollyon, which some Bible scholars interpret to be the Antichrist figure, Saddam cannot be the Antichrist, as the Antichrist should remain alive until Jesus returns. Therefore, the Gulf War cannot be the fifth trumpet. Of course, as this view, that Abaddon is the Antichrist, is just one of the many conjectures on the identity of Abaddon, one cannot assert that Saddam is not Abaddon for certain.

There are other problems when the Gulf War is associated with the fifth trumpet. The Gulf War incident lasted longer than five months; in actuality it lasted for about seven months. Remember, the power is given to the locusts to hurt men but it is limited to five months' duration. Apparently, the Gulf War cannot be the fifth trumpet.

Lastly, people were actually killed by the helicopters in the Gulf War. If the armed helicopters are interpreted as the locusts as some argue, then, according to the prophecies, the armed helicopters are only allowed to torment people like a scorpion. Even though the Bible indicates that the severity of the torment will be so great that people shall seek to rather die, the prophecy further specifies that death will escape them. In contrary to the specifics prophesied, the estimated civilian fatalities are 3,664 and the military fatalities between 20,000 and 26,000.[4] Therefore, the chance of Gulf War being the fulfillment of the fifth trumpet is out of the question.

What is more, the Gulf War occurred in 1990. Should Gulf War be the fifth trumpet, it should occur later than the fourth trumpet, Global Dimming. But as discussed in the previous chapter, Global

Dimming was fulfilled circa 2000. This precludes the Gulf War from being the fifth trumpet.

The Iraq War and the Abu Ghraib Torture?

On a similar note, some people propose that the fifth trumpet is the Iraq War that began on March 20, 2003. Their primary reason for this argument is the presence of the Abu Ghraib prison where the coalition forces arrested any Iraqi rebel suspects and held them for interrogation that involved abuse, torture, rape, sodomy, and homicide.[5] The proponents of this interpretation argue that such violence actually occurred for five months only, but this fact is not verifiable by any documentation.

The then President George Walker Bush declared war in 2003, and in 48 hours the USA attacked Iraq. A video on YouTube refers to this attack as the "star falling from heaven unto the earth."[6] The proposed interpretation is very intriguing, when one considers the fact that Baghdad is actually located in the land of ancient Babylonian Empire.

In the Scripture, locusts commanded to hurt, but not kill, men with power like scorpions appear. This power to torment them with the strike of locusts' stings is limited to five months' duration. The men desire to die, but death escapes them.

Could the locusts be the Apache helicopters in the Iraq War? The footages that show the Apache helicopters killing Iraqis exclude the possibility. [7] It is nearly impossible for Apache helicopters to only torture people and not take any lives in a war situation. Therefore, key features of the Iraq War render the incident disqualified as a possible interpretation for the fifth trumpet.

After the Iraqi regime collapsed, the Abu Ghraib prison became the US military prison, detaining up to several thousand prisoners. In 2003, the Abu Ghraib scandal became notorious after Dr. Abdel Salam Sidahmed, Deputy Director of Amnesty International's

Middle East Program, reported on human rights abuses by the US military at the Abu Ghraib prison. [8] This report led to an investigation of the army's prison system.

Major General Antonio M. Taguba's report says that "between October and December of 2003 there were numerous instances of 'sadistic, blatant, and wanton criminal abuses' at Abu Ghraib," including "breaking chemical lights and pouring the phosphoric liquid on detainees; pouring cold water on naked detainees; beating detainees with a broom handle and a chair; threatening male detainees with rape; allowing a military police guard to stitch the wound of a detainee who was injured after being slammed against the wall in his cell; sodomizing a detainee with a chemical light and perhaps a broom stick, and using military working dogs to frighten and intimidate detainees with threats of attack, and in one instance actually biting a detainee."[9] Graphic photos have been released to the public. Many have seen the photos—gruesome, cruel, and inhumane.

Revelation 9:7–9 describe the shapes of the locusts to be like horses prepared for battle, with crowns like gold on their heads, faces like the faces of men, having hair like that of women, and teeth like those of lions, having breastplates of iron, and the sound of their wings like the sound of chariots of many horses running to battle.

The Apache helicopters used in the Iraq War had the Longbow Fire Control Radar situated above the rotors. The advocates of the argument that the Iraq War is the fifth trumpet regard these radars to be the golden crowns. The Apache's front view in some ways resembles human face, with long propeller wings that spin looking like "women's hair." The Hellfire missiles somewhat look like the teeth of lions, and the helicopter wings do roar like the sound of chariots of many horses running to battle. No doubt, the helicopters are built with iron breastplates and have long tails like scorpions do. By stating that the Iraqis were tormented for five months, although the duration cannot be proven, the YouTube video mentioned above further argues that the Iraq War is the fifth trumpet.[10]

Yet, interpreting the Iraq War or the Abu Ghraib torture incident as the fifth trumpet raises questions. Although the US and coalition forces toppled Saddam Hussein's government in 2003, the insurgency against the US and coalition forces continued, and the war lasted until 2011. During this eight-year-long war, if the locusts exercised their power of scorpions only for a five months' period, are the locusts the helicopters or prison guards?

The locusts were not supposed to kill. Clearly, civilians died in the combat zones and prisoners in custody died.[11, 12] Also, the insurgents attacked the Abu Ghraib prison on April 20, 2004, killing twenty-two detainees and injuring ninety-two. [13] Apparently, the Iraq War and/or the Abu Ghraib torture incident(s) cannot be the candidates for the fifth trumpet.

What about the duration of the Abu Ghraib torture? Did it occur over five months? After the Abu Ghraib scandal came to public attention, the military inspection started in January of 2004. As already mentioned, the official report by Major General Antonio M. Taguba says that the abuses were between October and December of 2003. It means that the torture occurred for about two or three months long, obviously inconsistent with five months' duration as written in the Bible.

Human Rights Watch reported that: "U.S. General Sanchez announced on May 14, 2004, that he had barred the use of coercive interrogation techniques including 'stress positions,' 'sleep deprivation,' and the use of hoods, that had previously been available, though it is still not clear what he had previously approved." [14] The Abu Ghraib prison remained under the US military and coalition forces until 2006.[15] It is not known exactly how many months the detainees were tortured for, as some were detained for months and some over a year. It is not likely that they were tortured for five months, exactly one hundred and fifty days.

Lastly, if the Iraq War and the Abu Ghraib torture were the fifth trumpet, who would be the king of the locusts named Abaddon and Apollyon? If the king of the locusts was Saddam, then the king technically becomes the enemy of the locusts, not the commanding authority, as Apache helicopters were used by US military. As the locusts, Apache helicopters, belonged to the US military, the king of the locusts would have been the Commander-in-Chief of the US armed forces, the President of the United States, not Saddam Hussein.

With these unsettling questions, interpreting the Iraq War or the Abu Ghraib torture as the fifth trumpet becomes invalid.

Deepwater Horizon Oil Spill

What incident then would be the fifth trumpet? A recent oil rig explosion incident named Deepwater Horizon oil spill should be closely examined. A sea-floor oil gusher exploded on April 20, 2010 in the Gulf of Mexico, killing eleven workers and injuring seventeen.

According to BP, the estimated oil spill flow rate during this incident was "100,000 barrels (4.2 million gallons/15.9 million liters) of oil per day" in a worst case scenario.[16] This incident is regarded as the largest accidental maritime oil spill in history.

The oil rig explosion in the Gulf of Mexico itself was a disaster, but what made the incident even more devastating were the dispersants, Corexit 9527 and Corexit 9500, that were sprayed to break up the oil. The dispersants caused health hazards like in the days of the Gulf War, when the soldiers suffered "medically unexplained chronic multi-symptom illnesses" possibly from exposure to the nerve gas and depleted uranium. The illnesses the soldiers experienced were referred to as the Gulf War Syndrome.

After the oil rig incident, a new term called "New Gulf War Syndrome" came to birth.[17]

Fig. 7-1. Deepwater Horizon offshore drilling unit on fire. Photo courtesy of US Coast Guard.

The people in the Gulf of Mexico region who were exposed to the dispersants suffered strange disorders. The Corexit dispersant was "believed to be highly toxic—not just to marine life but also to the workers who were spraying it and locals living nearby."[18] The extensive spraying of the dispersant continued until mid-July, and the federal government officially declared successful permanent sealing of the oil well on September 19, 2010.

Before concluding the interpretation of the fifth trumpet as the Deepwater Horizon oil spill, there are several questions that must be examined. For fulfillment of the prophecy, the following features must be satisfied as discussed previously:

a) Smoke arises out of the pit.
b) There is a presence of locusts.
c) The locusts should not hurt the grass of the earth, neither any green thing, neither any tree.
d) The locusts torment men, but no one dies.
e) The locusts have power to torment men for five months.
f) The locusts have a king, whose name is Abaddon/Apollyon.

The rest of this chapter will walk through evidences of how the Deepwater Horizon oil spill incident fulfilled the aforementioned conditions.

a) Smoke arises out of the pit.

To discuss the first condition, let us read the relevant Scripture first:

> [Rev 9:1] And the fifth angel sounded, and I saw a star fall from heaven unto the earth: and to him was given the key of the *bottomless pit*.
> [Rev 9:2] And he opened the *bottomless pit*; and there arose a *smoke* out of the *pit*, as the *smoke* of a great furnace; and the sun and the air were darkened by reason of the *smoke* of the *pit*.

The corresponding Greek word for "bottomless" is ἄβυσσος (*abyssos*), a compound word formed with ἄ (*a*, first letter of Greek alphabet, "as a negative particle") and βυθός (*bythos*).[19] Βυθός (*bythos*) is defined as "the bottom or depth of the sea," or represents "the sea itself, the deep sea."[20] The Greek word φρέαρ (*phrear*) translated as the "pit" means "a well"[21] and was also used in the following verse:

> [Jn 4:11] The woman saith unto him, Sir, thou hast nothing to draw with, and the *well* (φρέαρ, *phrear*) is deep: from whence then hast thou that living water?

Combining the meanings together, the phrase, "the bottomless pit" (τὸ φρέαρ τῆς ἀβύσσου, *to phrear tēs abyssou*), therefore, means "the well of the very deep sea." The Scripture says the well in the deep ocean was "opened" (Rev 9:2), and smoke arose out of it.

An oil rig is a professional equipment used to drill holes and extract oil, many times in the floors of sea. At the time of the Deepwater Horizon oil spill incident, the oil rig was drilling a well at a water depth of 5,000 ft (1,500 m) when it caught fire on April 20, 2010.[22] The flame continued burning for over one full day and was quelled on April 22nd. The Coast Guard stated on CNN that the rig has gone under the water at approximately 10:21 a.m. on April 22, 2010.[23] These reports justifiably satisfy the prophecy of smoke arising out of the pit.

As described in Revelation 9:2, there was an opening of the bottomless pit at the Gulf of Mexico, and much smoke arose out of the pit like the smoke of a great furnace. The verse also describes that due to the smoke, the sun and the air were darkened (refer to Fig. 7-1).

After the explosion which caused the oil spill, the oil slicks were set on fire as a part of the clean-up operation as in Fig. 7-2. "Burning was implemented over nearly the full course of the DWH [Deepwater Horizon] event."[24] The "responders conducted 411 controlled burn events," and "burned 260,000 barrels (~11 million gallons) of oil *in situ*—5% of the total estimated release."[25]

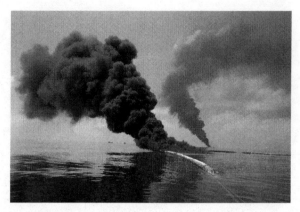

Fig. 7-2. Smoke and fire emerge as oil burns during a controlled fire in the Gulf of Mexico. Photo courtesy of US Navy.

The burning did not take place only at the original oil well site, but at multiple sites wherever the oil spread and drifted to. As a result, the smoke even reached the shorelines, leaving unpleasant black soot. In addition, the residents in the area became sick from breathing in the plume.

b) There is a presence of locusts.
Were there locusts involved in this BP Deepwater Horizon oil spill incident as described in Revelation chapter 9? If large amounts of the dispersants were sprayed with aircrafts every day, can these aircrafts be considered as the locusts?

The first piece of the puzzle must be resolved by determining whether these locusts are natural insects or not.

Let us examine the description of these locusts in Revelation:

> [Rev 9:11] And they had a *king* over them, which is the angel of the bottomless pit, whose name in the Hebrew tongue is Abaddon, but in the Greek tongue hath his name Apollyon.

A peculiar character of the said locusts is the presence of a king over them. As opposed to those locusts, the Scripture says that natural locusts have no king as follows:

[Pr 30:27] The locusts have *no king*, yet go they forth all of them by bands;

Is there a discrepancy in the Scripture if the Old Testament states that locusts have no king, while the New Testament writes of a king over them? Certainly not! The word of God is infallible and one can only deduce that there is a fundamental difference between these two types of locusts; the former are those of natural ones, the latter are those of non-natural origin. Therefore, Revelation must be describing certain characteristics of some other objects than real natural locusts.

When John described his vision, he would have used words available during the first century to describe the objects of the future. In other words, if John saw objects of modern era that did not exist during the first century, he would not know what names to call them. The only option for him to describe them would be using words that he knew.

Judging from the description of the locusts John provided, one can easily sense that they are not the ordinary creatures. Because they were distinct from what he had seen or known before, he put much effort into elaborating upon their characteristics. Having established that, let us read the following verse again and question what the locusts could be:

[Rev 9:3] And there came out of the smoke *locusts* upon the earth: and unto them was given power, as the scorpions of the earth have power.

In response to the explosion of the BP Deepwater Horizon drilling rig, more than 200 aircrafts were utilized. These included "from 70-year-old radial-engine DC-3s to a NASA ER-2, the agency's version of the high-flying U-2 spyplane." The aircrafts ranged from enormous to small size like Cessna of the Civil Air Patrol.[26]

Dispersant spraying operations were accompanied by planes that were equipped with various cameras, radars, and sensors that communicated with the commercial satellite to capture the image of oil and predict the spill's direction. The collected image data were sent to the spotter aircraft, which transmitted them to both of the dispersant spraying aircrafts and the oil skimming boats.[27]

Planes, ships, and boats were deployed to spray the dispersants. To spray the dispersants from the aircraft required high aviation technique, as spraying took place at a very low altitude, at around 50 feet to 150 feet. One of the planes used for spraying the Corexit dispersant was Basler BT-76 aircraft, which was specially modified DC-3 model. Four of the US Air Force C-130 Hercules aircrafts as well as other civilian Hercules aircraft were also utilized for dispersant spraying.[28]

A large aircraft like C-130 was used for spraying over big blocks of oil, whereas smaller aircrafts from civilian companies handled small patches of oil. These small aircrafts hopped around from one patch to the next as they traveled in the vast ocean. Long-range surveillance missions were carried out by the radar equipped HC-130 aircrafts of the US Coast Guard.[29]

When the Deepwater Horizon oil rig exploded on April 20, 2010, within thirty minutes, "five U.S. Coast Guard aircrafts took off from New Orleans and Mobile, Alabama, and headed to the scene."[30] The first dispersant spraying was done on April 22, 2010. The number of sorties to spray the dispersants increased fast as the participating aircrafts increased. It took less than a week to have about ten to fifteen sorties per day, reaching sometimes twenty after two weeks.[31]

The amount of dispersant sprayed increased as the oil continually gushed into the gulf. In the first week, the dispersant used already exceeded 100,000 US gallons, and in a month's time, the amount exceeded 600,000 US gallons. The entire operation involved complicated coordination between the military and civil air support missions:[32, 33]

> Oil flowed from the well for 87 days. Two drilling ships, numerous oil containment vessels, and a flotilla of support vessels were deployed to control the source of the well, while 835 skimmers and approximately 9,000 vessels were involved in the cleanup. On the single most demanding day of the response, over 6,000 vessels, 82 helicopters and 20 fixed wing aircrafts and over 47,849 personnel/responders were assigned; 88,522 square miles of fisheries were closed; 168 visibly oiled wildlife were collected; 3,795,985 feet of containment boom was deployed; 26 controlled in situ burns were conducted, burning 59,550 barrels of oil; 181 miles of shoreline were heavily to moderately oiled; 68,530 gallons (1,632 barrels) of dispersant were applied, and 27,097 barrels of oil were recovered.[34]

The response to the maritime ecological disaster involved numerous planes, as spraying missions generally required a spotter aircraft accompanying the dispersant spraying aircraft. Like this, there were many planes involved when the dispersants were sprayed.

The features of most of these aircrafts befit the peculiar descriptions of the locusts in Revelation. First, they have the shape of the locusts in flight with their wings spread. Second, all of the aircrafts have the breastplates of iron. Third, they made the noise resembling the horses prepared unto battle, due to the presence of propellers driven by combustive engines.

Fig. 7-3. A USAF C-130 tanker dumps dispersant over oil slicks caused by the BP oil spill disaster. Photo courtesy of USAF.

Interestingly, the aircraft models utilized for spraying the dispersants were propeller planes. If the incident were a true war, it would certainly have involved jets. However, during the BP Deepwater Horizon oil spill incident, the propeller planes were not engaged in any warfare, although they were actual military vessels and thus shaped as if "prepared unto battle" (Rev 9:7). These propeller planes most fit the descriptions of the locusts in Revelation and served as the main transporters of the dispersants, as well as the sprayers, as they were equipped to fly long-distance with slow speed as required for accurate targeted spraying.

The four of the puzzling descriptions of the locusts to interpret are (1) having the crowns like gold, (2) having the faces of men, (3) having the hair like that of women, and (4) having the teeth like those of lions. While multiple alternative views can exist in interpreting each description, the most probable interpretation is hereby presented.

Fig. 7-4. A US Coast Guard HC-130 Hercules aircraft.
Photo courtesy of US Navy.

The Scripture writes, "on their heads were as it were crowns like gold" (Rev 9:7). When John saw the locusts, most likely the dispersant spraying aircraft model C-130, he would have considered the front of its fuselage to be its "head." A modified variant of C-130 model, similar in the main features, is the US Coast Guard's HC-130 aircraft in Fig. 7-4. This aircraft probably headed to the scene right after the oil rig exploded, as it is a mainstay of the United States Coast Guard air fleet.[35]

Fig. 7-5. A C-130 Hercules aircraft seen from front.
Photo courtesy of USAF.

The C-130 aircraft has its defining features—a protruded front that looks like a nose and the front view that resembles a face of a man. The two small window panes situated above the "nose" would be perceived as its "eyes."

The part above these two windows, or the eyes, would be equivalent to the forehead. The description that there was a crown like gold on its head would mean that a certain shining object like gold, maybe a crown-shaped headband, wreathed its head portion. What could this be?

As explained in Volume 1, there are two kinds of crowns that appear in the Bible: a diadem (διάδημα, *diadēma*) primarily worn by kings, and the wreath (στέφανος, *stephanos*) usually given to the winner in a public game.[36] The "crowns" in Revelation 9:7 are originally the wreaths (στέφανοι, *stephanoi*), plural of στέφανος (*stephanos*), in Greek. Fig. 7-6 illustrates how the wreath was worn in Roman times. As clearly seen in the picture, the wreath is not sitting on the top of the head but worn around as if it encircles one's head.

Fig. 7-6. Latin Poet Ovid with his laurel wreath.[37]

Referring back to C-130 aircraft in the previous picture, Fig. 7-5, there is a long line of windows spanning across the entire forehead portion of its aircraft. The location corresponding to the cockpit of the aircraft is where the wreath would be worn as John described it. The cockpit windows will certainly shine as sun rays reflect off from different angles. Thus, a description of "as it were crowns [shining or reflecting light] like gold" (Rev 9:7).

In the previous discussion of the Iraq War as an unlikely candidate for the fifth trumpet, the argument that the Longbow Fire Control Radar situated above the rotors of the Apache helicopters "were as it were crowns like gold" was mentioned. However, the description of wreath (στέφανος, *stephanos*) excludes the possibility of the locusts being helicopters. The radar of Apache helicopter is located above the rotor and would have been described using the word diadem (διάδημα, *diadēma*). The diadem type of crown is seated on top of the head, not around, and would befit the description of the radar if the locusts were in fact helicopters. However, as the Scripture indicates the crowns were actually the wreath (στέφανος, *stephanos*), helicopters cannot be the locusts in Revelation.

If the head is on the front side of the aircraft, the teeth would be on the lower side of its head. Perhaps John wanted to describe the locusts as detailed as possible and discovered the presence of wheels on these aircrafts. In Fig. 7-4 and Fig. 7-5, two of C-130's front wheels are visible, as well as the side wheels near the wings' location. These wheels surface as the door opens during landing, and they are retracted behind the cover as the aircraft takes off. Such protrusion and retraction of wheels may have impressed John as teeth like lion's (Rev 9:8).

But why describe the wheels as the lion's teeth? When lion has his mouth closed, the daunting canines lurk within. When lion preys on animals, it uses those fangs that suddenly appear as mouth opens. Those carnassial blade-like teeth disappear into the mouth as it closes again.

Fig. 7-7. A male lion at a zoo yawning. Some of the teeth are visible.[38]

In a way, the wheels are like the lion's teeth in that they are not used at all times. Just as the canine teeth become visible or hidden during the hunting, the wheels come in and out of its compartments as the aircraft takes off or lands on the runway. Furthermore, the canine fangs are larger than the front teeth, just as the C-130's hind wheels are larger than the front wheels.

John probably witnessed how these aircrafts operate in detail. Perhaps from start to finish of the vision, John tried to provide important details that would serve as critical clues for future generations to interpret without mistakes. Without the description of lion's teeth, one may misinterpret these locusts to be helicopters, which do not have any parts such as wheels corresponding to lion's teeth that protrude from within at times.

Verse 8 writes these locusts also "had hair as the hair of women," which represent the propellers of the C-130 aircrafts. The blades of the propeller can be described as resembling the hair of women. Especially when the blades are in motion, the shape may be comparable to women's hair getting blown by the wind.

Such descriptions would be unsuitable if it were for the jets. Although the locusts looked "like unto horses prepared unto battle," there was actually no jet airplane flying around in the vicinity of the Gulf of Mexico. On the contrary, most of the aircrafts making flights during the operation were the propeller types except some, such as ER-2.

Hence, the descriptions in the prophecy clearly rule out jets and helicopters. In contrast, they precisely match the defining features of the dispersant spaying aircrafts C-130 of the Deepwater Horizon oil spill incident.

According to the prophecy, the locusts also had tails:

[Rev 9:10] And they had *tails* like unto scorpions, and there were stings in their *tails*: and their power was to hurt [the] men five months.

Both the tails and the stings are described, which are identifiable in Fig. 7-3. The chemical dispersant that comes out as "stings" from the ends of the "tails like unto scorpions" of the aircrafts harms those who breathe it.

Based on the observations thus far, the locusts in question can justifiably be interpreted as the dispersant spraying aircrafts that John saw in the Deepwater Horizon oil rig explosion incident.

Some may consider helicopters to be the locusts, as many of them actually flied during the clean-up operations. In fact, the FAA (Federal Aviation Administration) put temporary flight restrictions (TFR) in the region in order to free the helicopters and aircrafts from potential traffic hindrance.[39]

Fig. 7-8. Carolina locust in flight.[40]

But as discussed before, interpreting helicopters as the locusts is farfetched, especially because helicopters are devoid of wings, which the locusts must have as described in the Scripture:

> [Rev 9:9] And they had breastplates, as it were breastplates of iron; and the sound of their *wings* was as the sound of chariots of many horses running to battle.

As seen in Fig. 7-8, locusts in flight spread their wings to fullest extent. Such wing shape in motion resembles that of the plane rather than a copter. Missing wings eliminate helicopters from consideration.

Let us now read the descriptions of the locusts in their flight:

[Rev 9:3] And there came out of the smoke locusts *upon the earth* (εἰς τὴν γῆν, *eis tēn gēn*): and unto them was given power, as the scorpions of the earth have power.

The Scripture says that the locusts came "upon the earth." This description may seem contradictory to flying above the ocean, certainly "above the earth," while spraying the dispersant. To resolve this question, the original Greek expression needs to be understood. The expression "upon the earth" reads εἰς τὴν γῆν (*eis tēn gēn*), where the preposition εἰς (*eis*) is "denoting entrance into, or direction and limit: into, to, towards, for, among."[41]

This preposition is used in other parts of the Bible, such as in the following verse:

[Mt 4:18] And Jesus, walking by the sea of Galilee, saw two brethren, Simon called Peter, and Andrew his brother, casting a net *into the sea* (εἰς τὴν θάλασσαν, *eis tēn thalassan*): for they were fishers.

In the passage, Simon and Andrew cast their net into the sea. In other words, they throw it towards the sea. Other examples consistently show such usage of the preposition:

[Mt 2:1] Now when Jesus was born in Bethlehem of Judaea in the days of Herod the king, behold, there came wise men *from* (ἀπὸ, *apo*) the east *to* (εἰς, *eis*) Jerusalem,

This verse describes the wise men from the east traveling in the direction of Jerusalem. Conclusively, the preposition εἰς (*eis*) means "towards" that indicates direction.

Hence, the more accurate translation of the prophecy is rendered as follows:

[Rev 9:3] And there came out of the smoke locusts *towards* the earth: and unto them was given power, as the scorpions of the earth have power.

The passage is delineating how the locusts, or the aircrafts, flew towards the earth as they flew at low altitude to spray the dispersant. Then, why does the KJV write "there came locusts *upon* the earth" with a misused preposition? It is possibly because the translators back then only had understanding of locusts that dwell on land and therefore could hardly imagine locusts that fly low *towards* the earth.

Nonetheless, the passage clearly describes some flying objects, and the objects are not natural locusts. Natural locusts would fly off into the sky from earth, whereas the locusts in the passage fly towards the surface. As discussed before, the dispersants were unloaded at the altitude of 50 to 150 feet above the sea level. Therefore, the aircrafts flew at high altitude until they reached the oil spill regions, and only when it was time to spray the dispersant, they descended from heights "towards the ocean surface" to unload the chemicals. The Bible is astonishingly accurate in its descriptions!

Why then did the Scripture say the locusts flew towards the "earth" (γῆ, *gē*)? It is because the earth represents the planet where the land is, opposite from where the sky is. Accordingly, John expressed the aircrafts descending toward the surface of the earth, where the rising smoke originates, the sea. In doing so, John also made a clear distinction of the locusts from natural locusts that normally hop "on" or "in" the land, not fly "towards" (εἰς, *eis*).

c) The locusts should not hurt the grass of the earth, neither any green thing, neither any tree.

The *Huffington Post* reported in the article, *Corexit, Oil Dispersant Used By BP, Is Destroying Gulf Marine Life, Scientists Say,* as follows:

> But many scientists, such as Dr. William Sawyer, a Louisiana toxicologist, argue that Corexit can be deadly to people and sea creatures alike. "Corexit components are also known as deodorized kerosene," . . . "Studies of kerosene exposures strongly indicate potential health risks to volunteers, workers, sea turtles, dolphins, breathing reptiles and all species which need to surface for air exchanges, as well as birds and all other mammals." When Corexit mixes with and breaks down crude, it makes the oil far more "bioavailable" to plants and animals, critics allege, because it is more easily absorbed in its emulsified state.[42]

The Deepwater Horizon oil spill incident occurred only in the Gulf of Mexico. In the sea, the oil gushed out, upon which the dispersant was sprayed. Consequently, the creatures affected by this dispersant were primarily the marine life.

As verse 4 dictates "not to hurt the grass of the earth, neither any green thing, neither any tree," the fifth trumpet involves the ocean environment. Therefore, the conditions coincide with the situations of the BP Deepwater Horizon oil spill incident.

d) The locusts torment men, but no one dies.

If the BP Deepwater Horizon oil spill is indeed the fifth trumpet, then the locusts will appear out of the smoke and have the power like the scorpions to torment people for five months. The nature of torment would put people into severe discomfort but will not cause them to die.

Newsweek reported that people who worked at the BP oil disaster site in the Gulf of Mexico got ill: Jamie Griffin, a cook for the cleanup workers, was "coughing up blood and suffering constant headaches," and "lost her voice" within days. "Things got much worse," as time went by.[43]

Newsweek again reported that the mixture of crude and Corexit is dangerous: "The short-term health symptoms include acute respiratory problems, skin rashes, cardiovascular impacts, gastrointestinal impacts, and short-term loss of memory . . . Long-term impacts include cancer, decreased lung function, liver damage, and kidney damage."[44]

The article continues to say that:

> Nineteen months after the Deepwater Horizon explosion, a scientific study published in the peer-reviewed journal Environmental Pollution found that crude oil becomes 52 times more toxic when combined with Corexit . . . BP applied two types of Corexit in the gulf. The first, Corexit 9527, was considerably more toxic. According to the NALCO manual which provided Corexit, Corexit 9527 is an "eye and skin irritant. Repeated or excessive exposure . . . may cause injury to red blood cells (hemolysis), kidney or the liver." The manual adds: "Excessive exposure may cause central nervous system effects, nausea, vomiting, anesthetic or narcotic effects . . . Do not get in eyes, on skin, on clothing . . . Wear suitable protective clothing."[45]

The dispersant spraying operation compromised the health of many Gulf residents, causing them severe illnesses and suffering. Clayton Matherne, for example, a cleanup worker on the Gulf Coast, felt so sick that he prayed that "God will just let him die."[46]

Such accounts of severe suffering of the "New Gulf War Syndrome" can be viewed as a direct fulfillment of the prophecy, "shall men seek death, and shall not find it," in Revelation 9:6. No one has died from the actual spraying of Corexit, and "no death" signifies that the fifth trumpet is not a war. Again, a war such as Iraq War cannot be the fifth trumpet.

One might argue that eleven people were killed at the explosion on April 20, 2010, and thus the interpretation is implausible. However, the Scripture specifies the cause of the torment that makes people seek death unsuccessfully is the "stings in their [locusts'] tails," not the explosion. The Bible clearly writes that no one will be killed by the stings, the chemical dispersant coming out of the locusts. It does not state, and thus excludes, any other means of death. Therefore, the fatalities of the eleven people by the explosion do not contradict the description of the Scripture.

e) The locusts have power to torment men for five months.

In regards to the prophetic duration of five months, shall the Gregorian dates from April 20 (the day when the oil rig exploded) to September 19 (when the incident was declared resolved) be simply accepted as the five months' duration written in Revelation? Or is there a Biblical method of calculating days and time that would shed more light in figuring out the exact duration and clear any doubts and discrepancies?

Let us first consider how many days are in a Biblical month:

> [Gen 7:11] In the six hundredth year of Noah's life, in the *second month*, the *seventeenth day* of the month, the same day were all the fountains of the great deep broken up, and the windows of heaven were opened.
> [Gen 7:24] And the waters prevailed upon the earth *an hundred and fifty days*.

[Gen 8:4] And the ark rested in the *seventh month,* on the *seventeenth day* of the month, upon the mountains of Ararat.

The passage above clearly refers to 150 days' period—from the seventeenth of the second month to the sixteenth day of the seventh month—as the five months during which the water prevailed upon Earth. Only on the following day, the seventeenth of the seventh month, the ark rested upon the mountains. This account shows the number of days in a month in the Bible: 150 days/5 months renders thirty days per month.

Another Scripture, Revelation, affirms this premise:

[Rev 11:2] But the court which is without the temple leave out, and measure it not; for it is given unto the Gentiles: and the holy city shall they tread under foot *forty and two months.*
[Rev 12:6] And the woman fled into the wilderness, where she hath a place prepared of God, that they should feed her there *a thousand two hundred and threescore days.*
[Rev 12:14] And to the woman were given two wings of a great eagle, that she might fly into the wilderness, into her place, where she is nourished for *a time, and times, and half a time,* from the face of the serpent.

The forty-two months in Revelation 11:2 is equivalent to the 1,260 days written in Revelation 12:6, which is rephrased in verse 14 as "a time, and times, and half a time." Calculating 1,260 days/42 months yields 30 days per month. Since "a time, and times, and half a time" corresponds to 3.5 years, calculating 1,260 days/3.5 years also renders 360 days per year and 30 days per month. Detailed interpretation on chapters 11 and 12 of Revelation will be dealt with in later volumes.

Sir Isaac Newton stated that, "All nations, before the just length of the solar year was known, reckoned months by the course of the moon, and years by the return of winter and summer, spring and autumn; and in making calendars for their festivals, they reckoned thirty days to a lunar month, and twelve lunar months to a year, taking the nearest round numbers, whence came the division of the ecliptic into 360 degrees."[47]

In sum, in the Biblical calendar, there are consistently 30 days in a month and 360 days in a year, and 12 months in a year. Therefore, the five months' duration in Revelation 9:5 shall have no exception either.

The oil rig explosion incident started on April 20th and ended on September 19th. Based on these dates, the duration is not exactly five months, for there were 153 days in total. If the Bible reckons 42 months as exactly 1,260 days, then the five months shall be none other than 150 days.

According to the BP report, the response to the explosion was "the aerial application of dispersant in approximately 400 sorties, initiating use within 2 days of the spill."[48] This means, although the oil rig exploded on April 20th, BP did not start using the dispersant until two days later. But even if this two-day response time is subtracted from the 153 days, the duration is still a total of 151 days. This is a day longer than the five months in the Biblical calendar, where there are thirty days in each month. How can the seeming discrepancy be solved?

The answer comes from knowing which days to include in these five months and reviewing how to properly count the days amounting to five months. Regarding the start and finish of these five months, the Scripture writes:

> [Rev 9:5] And to them it was given that they should not kill them, but that they should be tormented *five months*: and their torment was as the torment of a *scorpion*, when he striketh a man.

[Rev 9:10] And they had tails like unto *scorpions*, and there were stings in their tails: and their power was to hurt [the] men *five months*.

During the five months the locusts have the power to torment. The torment clearly is caused by the locusts which strike men like the torment of a scorpion. Thus, the duration of the five months cannot be independent of the locusts.

In calculating the five months, the starting date of the duration must first be considered. Should it be when the smoke arose from the bottomless pit? Or is it when the locusts came out of the smoke upon the earth?

According to the Scripture, the beginning point cannot be the former, because, as discussed before, the five months are definitely related to the locusts and their tails that sting. In the case of the Deepwater Horizon oil spill, the start of the five months is not when the oil rig exploded but when the dispersant was first sprayed.

What about the last date of the five months? One cannot expect everyone stung by the locusts to fall ill for exactly five months' duration. Some may suffer for a shorter duration, and others may be affected for a greater duration. Some may suffer more severely, while others may be comparably less vulnerable to the torment.

For these reasons, the five month calculation could turn out to be a moot question if the duration for which all affected people suffered was sought for. After the well was capped on July 15, 2010, there was virtually no further use of the dispersants. July 19, 2010 was the last date the dispersant application is conducted.[49] However, these dates cannot be used to calculate the five months' duration as explained below.

As the Scripture clearly specifies the five months' duration, there should be clearly identifiable starting and finishing points of this period. Therefore, the last day of this five months' period may be rather relevant to the official date when the incident was declared to be resolved. This is even more probable when considering that the locusts have the "power" (ἐξουσία, *exousia*) (Rev 9:3, 10) to torment men for five months. Note that men are not tormented for five months, but the locusts have the power to torment men for five months. The meaning of ἐξουσία (*exousia;* power) includes "the power of authority" and "the power of rule or government,"[50] which not only mean the ability to enforce but also refer more closely to the executive authority.

The last date for the military aircrafts to spray the dispersants was July 19, 2010. The spraying by the locusts ceased not because there was an order to cease but because "there were no more easy oil 'targets' to be sprayed"[51] from the sky. Remaining smaller patches of oil were dealt with by ships and boats.

The last day of spraying activity does not annul the power of the locusts, because the authority continued to be in place for them to spray at any hour the need arose. Therefore, the last day of the locusts' "power to torment" shall rightfully be the date when the oil spill incident was officially declared resolved, so that the authority given to the aircrafts to spray the dispersants was no longer in effect.

In the case of the Deepwater Horizon oil spill, the official start date of the spraying of the dispersants can be found in the US federal government records. A military document that recorded the date was submitted to the National Response Team. Since the military aircrafts were deployed for spraying the dispersants, there is no better source than the military document to verify the facts.

The military document specifies word-for-word that on April 22, 2010—Day 3: "Aircraft apply surface dispersants for the first time." In page 34 of this same document, more details on this operation follow:

> The Deepwater Horizon RP [Responsible Party] submitted its first request to use aerial dispersants to

the FOSC [Federal On-Scene Coordinator] at Morgan City, La. The FOSC preauthorized its use at approximately 1 p.m. on April 22, 2010, and the RRT [Regional Response Team] received notification a few hours later.[52]

From this, the verifiable facts are: the first ever authorization for using the aerial dispersants was issued around 1 p.m., and the first aerial application "began at 1700 [5 p.m., CDT, April 22, 2010] using 1,880 gallons of COREXIT 9527."[53]

The exact time the incident came to a full conclusion can be found in an article from the *Boston Globe* with the headline, *Blow-out BP well finally killed at bottom of Gulf*:

> The Development Driller III, which drilled the relief well and pumped the cement to seal the Macondo well, the source of the Deepwater Horizon rig explosion and oil spill, is seen in the Gulf Of Mexico, off the coast of Louisiana, Saturday, September 18, 2010, on the day the cementing was completed.[54]

The article specifically says that the sealing of the well was completed (no later than) on Saturday, September 18, 2010.

The main text of the article further writes:

> The federal government's point man on the disaster said Sunday BP's well "is effectively dead" and posed no further threat to the Gulf. [He] said a pressure test to ensure the cement plug would hold was completed at 5:54 a.m. CDT. [Central Daylight Time, September 19, 2010].[55]

Bear in mind that when God created the light in the very first day, God called the light "day" and the darkness "night." As

Genesis 1:5 writes, the evening and the morning were the first day. This is why a Biblical calendar day starts with a sunset and ends with a sunset, which occurs in the evening around 6 p.m. Jerusalem time.

The use of Jerusalem time is essential for any timeline calculation of Bible prophecy, because the time and history revolve around Israel in the Bible. Hence, all calculation of a day, a month, a year, and seasons should rightfully be based on Jerusalem time and the Biblical calendar, even for interpreting Revelation.

With the Biblical definition of a calendar day in mind, what conclusion can be reached? The dispersants were applied at 5 p.m. CDT on April 22nd for the first time. At this time in Jerusalem, Israel, eight-hours different from Central Daylight Time with Daylight Saving, it was 1 a.m. on April 23rd. It was also a new following day in the Biblical calendar, because it was already past 6 p.m. in Jerusalem. Furthermore, the FOSC preauthorized to use aerial dispersants at approximately 1 p.m. CDT on April 22nd, which corresponds to 9 p.m. on April 22nd in Jerusalem. It was also a new following day in Jerusalem time according to the Biblical calendar, as it was already past 6 p.m. in Jerusalem.

Complete sealing of the well was officially tested and confirmed at 5:54 a.m. on September 19th. Even with time difference, this was still within the same day in Israel according to the Biblical calendar.

Counting from the starting date to the last date results in exactly 150 days in all, exactly five months as written in Revelation 9:5, as it was one day shorter in Jerusalem time in the Biblical calendar, while it was 151 days in CDT in the Gregorian calendar.

The reason for proving the said five months to be exactly 150 days is because other dates in the Bible also count the exact number of days. As discussed before, the Scripture in Genesis specifies five months to be exactly 150 days, and Revelation writes 3.5 years to be 1,260 days. Since Revelation especially equates 42 months as exactly 1,260 days, the interpretation of the five months in the fifth trumpet shall not be 149 days nor 151 days, but exactly 150 days.

If the BP Deepwater Horizon oil spill incident is the fifth trumpet, all the facts presented in Revelation's descriptions must agree. Finally, the last puzzle remains for discussion.

f) The locusts have a king, whose name is Abaddon/Apollyon.

The king of the locusts is named Abaddon (אֲבַדּוֹן, 'abaddown) in Hebrew, the meaning of which is "(1) destruction, Job 31:12. (2) place of destruction, abyss [the bottomless pit], nearly synon. with שְׁאוֹל [shĕ'owl; hell], Job 26:6; 28:22; Pro. 15:11."[56]

> [Job 26:6] Hell (שְׁאוֹל, shĕ'owl) is naked before him, and destruction (אֲבַדּוֹן, 'abaddown) hath no covering.
>
> [Job 26:6] γυμνὸς ὁ ᾅδης (hades; hell) ἐπώπιον αὐτοῦ καὶ οὐκ ἔστιν περιβόλαιον τῇ ἀπωλείᾳ (apoleia; destruction) (LXX)

The noun ἀπωλεία (apoleia) translated as destruction is related to the verb "ἀπόλλυμι (apollumi)" which means "to destroy fully."[57] Therefore, the Greek name Ἀπολλύων (Apollyōn) shares the same meaning of destruction, which appears together with the word "hell" (ᾅδης, hades) that is related to the abyss, the bottomless pit.

The prophecy says that there is a king, who is the angel of the bottomless pit, whose orders the locusts follow. The king has the name of Abaddon in Hebrew tongue and Apollyon in Greek tongue, and its meaning in English is "destroyer." There is nobody named Abaddon, Apollyon, or Destroyer, but as much as these names are symbolic, some inferences can also be made based on this symbolic reference.

The BP Deepwater Horizon oil spill is recorded as one of the worst manmade environmental disasters in the US and world history. Judging from its extensive negative and destructive impact on the lives and ecosystem in the Gulf of Mexico, "destroyer" is well suited for the king's title at the least.

The Scripture provides two names: Abaddon in the Hebrew tongue and Apollyon in the Greek tongue. This suggests that the name in question is not an actual name, but a symbolic reference to defining characteristics of the person. If it were an actual name, only one reading or similar pronunciation would have been provided.

Some readers might ask the following challenging question: why is the name of the king of the locusts in the fifth trumpet interpreted as symbolic, when the name Wormwood for the star in the third trumpet was interpreted to literally represent the city Chernobyl?

> [Rev 8:11] And the *name of the* (ὄνομα τοῦ, *onoma tou*) star is called Wormwood: and the third part of the waters became wormwood; and many men died of the waters, because they were made bitter.

The answer to this question is found in the Scripture regarding the name of the angel of the bottomless pit in Greek:

> [Rev 9:11] And they had a king over them, which is the angel of the bottomless pit, *whose name* (ὄνομα αὐτῷ, *onoma autō*; a name to him) in the Hebrew tongue is Abaddon, but in the Greek tongue hath his name Apollyon.

In this verse, the part translated as "whose name . . . is Abaddon" is written originally as "a name to him (ὄνομα αὐτῷ, *onoma autō*) . . . Abaddon."[58] Αὐτῷ (*autō*) is in the dative form, when directly translates, reads "to him," indicating that the use of the dative form renders it possible for the name to be an appellation representing the characteristic of the person, although it can be used when an actual name is given at birth. Such expression differs from the genitive form "ὄνομα τοῦ" (*onoma tou*), which directly translates to "name of the" as written in KJV regarding the name of the Wormwood in the third trumpet. Moreover, "a name to him [the king]" strongly implies that the name is given to him when he is in office rather than when he is born. In the case of Abaddon, therefore, the use of the dative form renders it more likely that the name is an appellation given to the king over the locusts, rather than a real name.

Another example in Revelation affirms how a dative form is used to give a name to represent the character:

> [Rev 6:8] And I looked, and behold a pale horse: and *his name* (ὄνομα αὐτῷ, *onoma autō*) that sat on him was Death, and Hell followed with him. And power was given unto them over the fourth part of the earth, to kill with sword, and with hunger, and with death, and with the beasts of the earth.

In this verse also, the expression "his name . . . was Death" in original Greek is written as "a name to him (ὄνομα αὐτῷ, *onoma autō*) . . . was Death." Clearly, "Death" is not the real name of the rider of a pale horse but a characterization of his symbolic traits.

In brief, the "destroyer" would be the characterization of a person rather than the actual autonym. Some more examples in the Scripture testify to these cases:

> [Mk 3:17] James the [son] of Zebedee and John the brother of James, *to whom* (αὐτοῖς, *autois*) He gave the *name* (ὄνομα, *onoma*) Boanerges, that is, "Sons of Thunder"; (NKJV)

Here, dative form is used again for "to whom" when appellation is given after their characteristics.

Of course, even the genitive form can be used, as seen below, for the name to portray the features of the beings:

> [Mk 5:9] And he asked him, What is *thy name* (σοι ὄνομά, *soi onoma*)? And he answered, saying, *My name* (ὄνομα μοι, *onoma moi*) is Legion: for we are many.

However, as the uses of the dative form in various Scriptures abovementioned suggest, the name in the dative form in Revelation 9:11 given to the king over the locusts when in office, not at his birth, most likely indicates that Abaddon is an appellation and describes his characteristics.

Since the locusts physically follow the order of a commander, it suffices to say that the king of the locusts bears an actual physical form. Then, who might be this king of the locusts? Can he be the actual commander-in-chief of the mobilized military units? Or, can he be some hidden figure with political power of great magnitude that allows him to orchestrate the disaster related clean-up activities on a grand scale?

The "king" or the "commander-in-chief" of the locusts is clearly defined in the US Constitution, according to the Department of Defense article:

> Defense Secretary Donald Rumsfeld put out a memo Oct. 24 to DoD [Department of Defense] leaders saying there is only one commander in chief in America -- the president.
> His memo also forbids use of the acronym "CINC" (pronounced "sink") with titles for military officers.
> The title of commander in chief is enshrined in the U.S. Constitution. Article II, Section 2, states, "The President shall be Commander in Chief of the Army

and Navy of the United States, and of the Militia of the several States, when called into the actual Service of the United States."

Even before World War II, however, the title was applied to U.S. military officers, and over the years "commander in chief" came to refer to the commanders of the U.S. unified combatant commands. Their titles became, for instance, "Commander in Chief, U.S. Pacific Command" or "Commander in Chief, U.S. Transportation Command."

No more. Rumsfeld has been using the term "combatant commander" for months now when referring to a regional organization such as the U.S. Central Command and "commander" when talking about a specified unit such as the U.S. Strategic Command.[59]

As the locusts belonged to the US military, the king of the locusts would be the Commander-in-Chief of the US armed forces, the President of the United States at the time—Barack Hussein Obama II. In fact, Fox News wrote regarding the depiction of the then President Obama as Lord Shiva on the cover page of *Newsweek* on November 22, 2010 as follows:

The Newsweek cover shows Obama with several arms carrying policy issues while balancing on one leg. The headline reads: "God of All Things" with a subtitle, "Why the Modern Presidency May be too Much for One Person to Handle."

Shiva, who is one of three pre-eminent gods in the Hindu religion along with Brahma and Vishnu, is considered the destroyer of the world, which must end, metaphorically speaking, in order to be reborn as a more universalistic place.[60]

David Limbaugh, in his book entitled *The Great Destroyer: Barack Obama's War on the Republic* published in 2012, states:

> When it comes to our prosperity, our freedom tradition, and our constitutional government, President Barack Obama has been the great destroyer-- knocking down the free-market economy and principles of limited government that have made America the envy of the world . . . the Obama administration has waged a relentless, nearly four-year-long war to transform our nation into a country where federal bureaucrats have more power over our lives than we do; where leftist crony capitalism dependent on government subsidies is replacing the real thing; where, in an Orwellian inversion of meaning, a savagely weakened national defense somehow makes us stronger and trillions in deficit spending on counterproductive government "stimulus" and welfare programs somehow makes us richer.[61]

An article from Right Wing Watch written in June 2014 says that the then President Obama is "the chosen destroyer of America":

> Obama doesn't have a dream to destroy America and make her disappear, but rather to enslave, control, and manipulate the people and all our assets. All those who resist his agenda will be destroyed . . . We see Obama organizing and enforcing a tectonic shift through the Islamic lead caliphate, with the goal of controlling the entire world one day. We have watched Obama side with Islamic dictator after dictator—exposing again and again his real faith in Allah and Muhammad, not the Holy Bible and Jesus

Christ. Think of the endless amount of corrupt and criminal dictators and terrorist groups he has boldly backed—Zelaya, Morsi, giving aid, and comfort to the Taliban, employing Muslim Brotherhood members through out his staff on and on it goes. He always sides against the Christians and Jews and for Islamic radicals.[62]

Another article from *American Thinker* written on November 15, 2016 entitled *Obamacare the Destroyer: How It Has Hurt Small Business* writes: "We have lost so much—not just as a company. Our nation has wasted eight years with this vain and costly experiment in statist coercion. It has stalled our economy . . ."[63]

If the interpretation that the BP Deepwater Horizon oil spill is the fifth trumpet is correct, the king of the locusts must be the President of the United States at the time. The Scripture says that the king of the locusts is given the name of Abaddon/Apollyon, meaning the destroyer. It is interesting to see that the former President Obama has been called the Destroyer in many aspects, from economics to religious standpoints. Could this appellation given to him prove the fulfillment of the Scripture in Revelation 9:11?

The answer would be yes, only if the interpretation of the BP Deepwater Horizon oil spill as the fifth trumpet is correct. However, whether the Abaddon/Apollyon is the Antichrist-to-be or not is a separate matter. In other words, the fact that the former President Obama is the king of the locusts in the fifth trumpet does not automatically lead to the conclusion that Obama is the Antichrist-to-be.

Is Abaddon (Apollyon) the Antichrist?

Then comes the question—is Abaddon (Apollyon) the Antichrist? In fact, very rarely would a person be given a name meaning "destroyer" at birth. As addressed before, Saddam Hussein's first name is often interpreted to mean the "destroyer," but he cannot be the Antichrist, for he has already died. More importantly, he cannot be the king of the locusts in the fifth trumpet, as many people were killed during Saddam's Gulf War or Iraq War. The Scripture, however, says that no one should lose life due to the locusts during this event.

As already discussed before, there is a perspective that Abaddon/Apollyon is no other than the Antichrist and thus the beast. This perspective has been established based on the following Scriptures:

> [Rev 9:11] And they had a king over them, which is the *angel of the bottomless pit*, whose name in the Hebrew tongue is Abaddon, but in the Greek tongue hath his name Apollyon.
> [Rev 11:7] And when they shall have finished their testimony, the *beast* that ascendeth out of the *bottomless pit* shall make war against them, and shall overcome them, and kill them.

The beast is the Antichrist, who rises up out of the sea as in the following verse. For this reason, the inference has been made that the sea and the abyss (bottomless pit) are related.

> [Rev 13:1] And I stood upon the sand of the sea, and saw a *beast* rise up out of the *sea*, having seven heads and ten horns, and upon his horns ten crowns, and upon his heads the name of blasphemy.

Tracing back to Revelation 9:11, another inference has been made that it is probable that the king of the locusts, who is the angel of the bottomless pit, is the Antichrist, because Abaddon is related to the bottomless pit (abyss).

[Rev 17:8] The *beast* that thou sawest was, and is not; and shall ascend out of the *bottomless pit*, and go into perdition: and they that dwell on the earth shall wonder, whose names were not written in the book of life from the foundation of the world, when they behold the *beast* that was, and is not, and yet is.

As mentioned before, the angel of the bottomless pit appears in Revelation 9:11 at the fifth trumpet. In Revelation chapter 11 toward the end of the sixth trumpet, this powerful beast that ascended out of the bottomless pit kills the "two witnesses." Then in Revelation 17 as one of the angels which had the seven bowls full of God's wrath explains about the judgment of the "Mystery, Babylon the Great, the Mother of Harlots and Abominations of the Earth," the angel also explains in verse 8 that the beast that ascended out of the bottomless pit will go into perdition.

According to the perspective that Abaddon/Apollyon is the Antichrist, one can connect the dots from these verses that the angel of the bottomless pit (Rev 9:11) is the beast who ascends out of the bottomless pit (Rev 11:7), and that this one man who is the Antichrist that ascends out of the bottomless pit (Rev 17:8) rules from the time of the fifth trumpet until the end of final seven-year period.

However, one cannot identify who this beast out of the bottomless pit is until he actually rises to power in the middle of the final seven-year period to claim himself to be god and enforces the mark of the beast on the right hands or the foreheads of all people.

There is always probability that the angel of the bottomless pit in Revelation 9:11 is not the Antichrist, even though the word "sea" in Revelation 13:1 is related to the abyss. The identity of the Antichrist cannot be absolutely affirmed at this time of July 2018, because the Seven-Year Treaty has not been signed yet. The one who confirms the Seven-Year Covenant is the Antichrist-to-be, who will set up the abomination that causes desolation in the midst of the final seven years:

> [Da 9:27] And he shall confirm the *covenant* with many for *one week*: and in the *midst of the week* he shall cause the sacrifice and the oblation to cease, and for the overspreading of *abominations* he shall make it desolate, even until the consummation, and that determined shall be poured upon the desolate.

Let us now assume that Abaddon in Revelation chapter 9 is the Antichrist-to-be. As will be discussed in chapter 9 of this volume, Revelation chapter 10 writes of the Seven-Year Covenant. If the fifth trumpet had already been blown in 2010, and if Abaddon in Revelation chapter 9 (the fifth trumpet) and the Antichrist-to-be in Revelation 11:7 are identical, then it would mean that the person to be the Antichrist is alive and active from time of the fifth trumpet until the end of the final seven years.

This volume will not specifically identify who the Antichrist is. But as explored thus far, if the king Abaddon from the fifth trumpet is the Antichrist-to-be, he already exists here on Earth. Needless to say, he is the one who held the power to command the locusts to action. Readers can by themselves figure out who this might be as the necessary information is provided.

A daunting factor about the incident in the Gulf of Mexico is that it may not entirely be a spontaneous accident. This is suggested as a 2009 Hollywood movie titled *Knowing* predicted and showed the almost exact scene of the accident in the Gulf of Mexico, a year prior to the actual accident.

More surpassing in power and foreknowledge than a movie is indeed God, who prophesied this incident nearly two thousand years ago and ensures that the prophecy is actually carried out in physical form as written in the Bible. God has forewarned that these prophetic events are only the beginning.

The identity of Abaddon or Apollyon, the angel of the bottomless pit that possibly becomes and rules as the Antichrist, still needs some time to be affirmed. Yet, right after providing the name of the king over the locusts, the Bible clearly forewarns the saints to pay attention to the fifth trumpet by stating that the first woe of the three is past:

> [Rev 9:12] One *woe* is past; and, behold, there come two *woes* more hereafter.

Woe is an expression of grief. Why does God specify this event as one woe? What characteristic of the fifth trumpet makes the event a woeful incident? In fact, after the fourth trumpet is completed, the Bible writes:

> [Rev 8:13] And I beheld, and heard an angel flying through the midst of heaven, saying with a loud voice, *Woe, woe, woe,* to the inhabiters of the earth by reason of the other voices of the trumpet of the three angels, which are yet to sound!

Among the twenty-one prophetic events of seals, trumpets, and bowls, God has designated only the last three trumpets as "woes." Compared to the first and second trumpets that occupied years in duration, the fifth trumpet only lasted five months, let alone no one died. Yet, it is still labeled a "woe." Why?

The reason most likely relates to the Antichrist figure. Not only the fifth trumpet but also the sixth and the seventh trumpet are related to (the rise of) the Antichrist. This is, of course, if the identity of Abaddon or Apollyon is indeed the Antichrist. The greatest woe for humanity is the rise of the Antichrist, who will appear at the climax of such disastrous events and is related to the devil:

> [Rev 12:12] Therefore rejoice, ye heavens, and ye that dwell in them. *Woe* to the inhabiters of the earth and of the sea! for the *devil* is come down unto you, having great wrath, because he knoweth that he hath but a short time.

When the seventh trumpet, the third woe, is sounded, the Antichrist finally calls himself god while making all small and great, rich and poor people receive the mark of the beast in the right hands or in the foreheads.

Given that Abaddon or Apollyon of the fifth trumpet is the Antichrist, the woes begin with the appearance of the Antichrist-to-be on the political stage in the fifth trumpet, and continue until the Antichrist calls himself god.

Having established that Abaddon or Apollyon may be the Antichrist, it is important to note that this being is also described as "the angel of the bottomless pit" in Revelation 9:11. An angel (ἄγγελος, *aggelos*; "a messenger; especially an 'angel'"[64]) most of the times denotes a spiritual being in the book of Revelation from chapter 5 and on. Thus, based on the expression, "the angel of the bottomless pit," it is not certain whether Abaddon is a human being or not. If Abaddon, the king of the locusts, is a spiritual being, then he cannot be the Antichrist-to-be, who would definitely be a human being. However, as the locusts are actual physical entities, their king is also most likely a human being rather than a spiritual being.

Therefore, readers must keep watch and discern the times and be prepared to make accurate assessment as the prophetic time and events unfold before the eyes and as the Antichrist rises to power to rule the world as a dictator.

The Seal of God

Lastly, let us examine the Scripture about "the seal of God."

[Rev 9:4] And it was commanded them that they should not hurt the grass of the earth, neither any green thing, neither any tree; but only those men which have not the *seal of God* in their foreheads.

During the fifth trumpet, it was the Corexit dispersants that tormented people and Revelation writes that the people tormented would have been only those without the seal of God in their foreheads.

Why would God care to write in Revelation, or more specifically only in the description for the fifth trumpet out of all the twenty-one seal, trumpet, and bowl events prophesied in Revelation, to show discrimination between those sealed by God and those without the seal of God? This must be God's special way of warning the readers that the time is approaching when this difference in spiritual standing will make a huge apparent difference in the outcome.

The third of mankind will be slayed during the sixth trumpet, and the rapture will occur at the seventh trumpet. There are also the seven bowls full of God's wrath and the subsequent final war! There are ongoing events waiting in series for the humanity, but who comes out unscathed will depend on whether he or she is known by God or not.

As discussed in chapter 1, the "ones having the seal of God" are those saved by faith in Christ. How can an untargeted, indiscriminate spraying of dispersant only hurt "those men which have not the seal of God?" Could this incident actually be a spiritual one?

There are similar scenes recorded in the Bible, having to do with God's special demarcation:

[Eze 9:4] And the LORD said unto him, Go through the midst of the city, through the midst of Jerusalem, and set a *mark* upon the foreheads of the men that sigh and that cry for all the abominations that be done in the midst thereof.

[Eze 9:5] And to the others he said in mine hearing, Go ye after him through the city, and smite: let not your eye spare, neither have ye pity:

[Eze 9:6] Slay utterly old and young, both maids, and little children, and women: but come not near any man upon whom is the *mark*; and begin at my sanctuary. Then they began at the ancient men which were before the house.

In the passage above, God showed Ezekiel a vision, in which righteous men of God were marked on their foreheads. The calamity that followed only fell on those who did not have the marks. The scene exhibits how the spiritual sealing of God manifests in a tangible physical end result. There is another similar scene:

[Eze 12:13] My net also will I spread upon him, and he shall be taken in my snare: and I will bring him to Babylon to the land of the Chaldeans; yet shall he not see it, though he shall die there.

[Eze 12:14] And I will scatter toward every wind all that are about him to help him, and all his bands; and I will draw out the sword after them.

[Eze 12:15] And they shall know that I am the LORD, when I shall scatter them among the nations, and disperse them in the countries.

[Eze 12:16] But I will leave a few men of them from the sword, from the famine, and from the pestilence; that they may declare all their abominations among the heathen whither they come; and they shall know that I am the LORD.

In the passage, God determines to scatter Israelites into all directions and have the sword chase after them. In the end, those who survived the sword will be left to declare the abominations among the heathen. In other words, God speaks of an event that would purge those who will not "acknowledge all their detestable practices." (NIV)

In sum, the spiritual sealing of God could result in different physical finale, and the case of Deepwater Horizon oil rig explosion is no exception.

Interpretation of the BP Deepwater Horizon oil spill as the fifth trumpet had already been proclaimed on the authors' YouTube channel in 2011. In this regard, the authors may be one of the first to interpret the fifth trumpet as the BP Deepwater Horizon oil spill.

CHAPTER 8.
THE SIXTH TRUMPET:
THE FOUR ANGELS
TO SLAY THE THIRD PART OF MEN

As discussed in the previous chapter, the last three trumpets are described as "woes" (Rev 8:13). The first woe is the fifth trumpet, the second woe the sixth trumpet, and the third woe the seventh trumpet.

The completion of the fifth trumpet is declared in Revelation 9:12, where the Scripture states, "The first woe is past." The sixth trumpet, the second woe, starts when the sixth angel sounds his trumpet in Revelation 9:13. The sixth trumpet is declared completed when the Scripture writes "The second woe has passed" in Revelation 11:14, after the two witnesses in Revelation 11 ascend up to heaven in a cloud. In this regard, the period of the sixth trumpet includes World War III in Revelation 9:13–21, and "a little book" and "the seven thunders" in Revelation chapter 10, as well as the period of the two witnesses prophesying in Revelation 11:3–13. In this chapter, only WWIII is discussed. The two witnesses of Revelation 11 will be discussed in the next volume.

Intervals of the Trumpets

As was discussed in the previous volume, the intervals of the seals showed a trend, and likewise, the intervals of the trumpets also show a certain trend. In 1914, the first trumpet was sounded, and in 1939, the second trumpet, which are World War I and II, respectively. The third trumpet, the Chernobyl nuclear disaster, was sounded in 1986. The fourth trumpet, the Global Dimming phenomenon, was sounded around the end of the twentieth century. The fifth trumpet, the BP Deepwater Horizon oil spill incident, was sounded in 2010.

From the first to the second trumpet, there was 25-year lapse of time. The next trumpet was sounded 47 years afterwards, after a longer interval. But since then, the interval seems to be shortening, quickening the occurrence of subsequent trumpet events, and hence, mimicking the frequency of birth pangs (ὠδίν, ōdin).[1] The word ὠδίν (ōdin) used to denote birth pangs is used in the following verses:

> [Mk 13:8] For nation shall rise against nation, and kingdom against kingdom: and there shall be earthquakes in divers places, and there shall be famines and troubles: these are the beginnings of sorrows (ὠδίν, ōdin).
> [1Th 5:3] For when they shall say, Peace and safety; then sudden destruction cometh upon them, as travail (ὠδίν, ōdin) upon a woman with child; and they shall not escape.

If the percentage of women experiencing contractions since the time of pregnancy is graphed against pregnancy weeks, the probability of contractions occurring increases exponentially as weeks go by in pregnancy.[2] The contractions exist from the early stages of pregnancy, and occur more frequently as childbirth

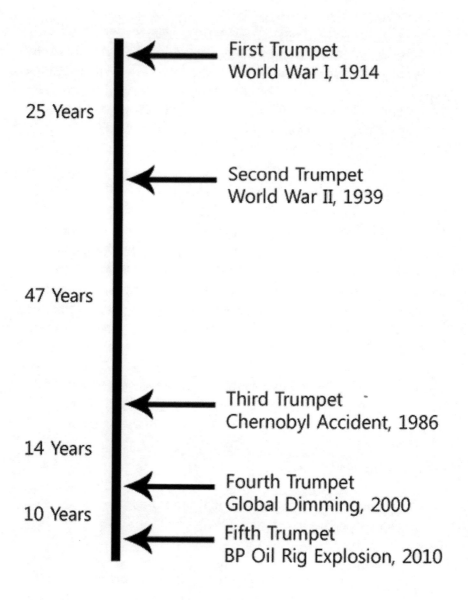

Fig. 8-1. Intervals of the trumpets.

nears. The birth pangs are associated with the frequent contractions toward the last stages of pregnancy, near childbirth. As Jesus answers His disciples' question regarding the end of the world (Mt 24:3; Mk 13:4), He uses the word "birth pangs." The seals are probably comparable to the contractions of the early and middle stages of pregnancy, and the trumpets and the bowls to those of the last stages, thus the birth pangs.

Usually, when a woman becomes pregnant, she hardly experiences any contractions in the beginning. But toward the end of her pregnancy, as the time for childbirth approaches, she starts experiencing birth pangs associated with more frequent contractions. The first and second birth pangs might come with few days apart. The birth pangs would then start to come every day, then every hour, then every minute, and finally, continuously at the time of delivery.

This is how the intervals of contractions shorten during pregnancy leading to childbirth, and this is how the prophetic events of Revelation will unfold. The seven seals unfolded in centurial intervals. The seven trumpets would unfold in decadal intervals. The seven bowls would all be poured in intervals less than a year as all seven of them will be poured within the last 3.5 years.

The Scale of the War

The event to be interpreted next is the sixth trumpet, which has not been sounded yet to date (July 2018). Regarding WWIII of the sixth trumpet, Revelation writes as follows:

[Rev 9:13] And the sixth angel sounded, and I heard a voice from the four horns of the golden altar which is before God,

[Rev 9:14] Saying to the sixth angel which had the trumpet, Loose the four angels which are bound in the great river Euphrates.

[Rev 9:15] And the four angels were loosed, which were prepared for an hour, and a day, and a month, and a year, for to slay *the third part of* [*the*] *men*.

[Rev 9:16] And the number of the army of the horsemen were two hundred thousand thousand: and I heard the number of them.

[Rev 9:17] And thus I saw the horses in the vision, and them that sat on them, having breastplates of fire, and of jacinth, and brimstone: and the heads of the horses were as the heads of lions; and out of their mouths issued fire and smoke and brimstone.

[Rev 9:18] By these three was *the third part of* [*the*] *men* killed, by the fire, and by the smoke, and by the brimstone, which issued out of their mouths.

If the sixth trumpet is examined in the original Greek text, verse 15 reads: "the third part of [the] men." There is the definite article "the" in front of "men." The same expression in verse 18 also contains "the" in front of "men" in the original Greek text. But since many Bible translations, including the King James Version, omitted this definite article "the" in their translations, some have interpreted that the third of the entire mankind on Earth are to be killed during this event. A third of the world population in 2016 is about 2.5 billion. Of course this is possible, but there are at least two more possible interpretations.

First, the number could be the third of the "two hundred thousand thousand" soldiers deployed for the war (Rev 9:16). Second, it can be the third of the total population of the countries that participate in the war. Either way, the death toll from the war should reach a minimum of 66.6 million, which is one third of "two hundred thousand thousand" soldiers. On the other hand, it could mean that the two hundred million soldiers will go about killing the third of the population in the war zones or the entire world. In any case, judging from the astounding death toll, this incident must be nothing but World War III.

What could be the maximum number of fatalities? Although the definite article is present, as there is no phrase that modifies or specifies "the men" (verse 15) prior to the expression, "the men" may also be referring to the general world population. Thus, a maximum of one third of the world population may be killed in this event.

A more in-depth analysis is called for. There were just over one hundred million soldiers mobilized for the Second World War.[3] The "two hundred thousand thousand" (or two hundred million) in the sixth trumpet most probably refers to the number of mobilized soldiers. Having said this, the Scripture is signifying that WWIII will recruit more men than in the time of WWII and that WWIII will definitely be a larger scale of war.

If the interpretations on the first and second trumpets as WWI and WWII are correct, then an interesting discovery can be made. The Scripture does not include any expressions of direct reference to men dying nor quote any number of deaths incurred in the prophecies of the first two world wars. In the descriptions of WWI, only the earth, trees, and all green grass were devastated, although there is an implicit expression that men died of "hail and fire mingled with blood." In the descriptions of WWII, the third part of the creatures in the sea became blood, but there was no direct mention of "men" in the prophecy.

In contrast, during the sixth trumpet, the four angels prepared for slaying the third part of the "men" are loosed. In fact, death of the "third part of [the] men" is mentioned two times in the verses 15 and 18. Such reiteration may be a way of emphasizing that many lives will be lost as a result. Consequent inference allows speculation of extreme count on death toll ensued from WWIII.

The total estimate of fatalities from WWI is about 15 million, and from WWII is 50 million or a bit more. Some sources reveal that the death toll of WWII reaches about 66 million,[4] which is about 3 percent of the world population then, assuming that the world population then was 2.3 billion.[5]

In WWII, vast majority of the nations were involved in the war. In WWIII, even more number of nations is expected to participate in the war. Compared to the high estimate death toll of 66 million from WWII, larger death toll is expected from WWIII. Therefore, the "third part of [the] men" in Revelation 9:15 may well be over a mere one third of 200 million, or 66.6 million, a number comparable to the death toll of WWII. Following this logic, the Scripture is most likely referring to the third part of the world population being killed in WWIII of the sixth trumpet.

When interpreting the seals in the previous volume, studying history revealed that during the fourth seal, Genghis Khan's Mongol Invasion had annihilated 11.1 percent of the world population then. During the fourth seal, power was given only over the fourth part of the earth, yet over 10 percent of world population was affected then. If the percentage of the world population reduction by Mongol Invasion incident, 11.1 percent, was applied to today's statistics, more than 800 million people would have died. In this sense, WWIII, exceedingly larger in scale than Mongol Invasion, may as well surpass 800 million in death toll, reaching the third of the world population.

The Horses

The "horses" described in the sixth trumpet perhaps refer to missile systems. The following verses portray their features and how these weapons kill people.

[Rev 9:17] And thus I saw the horses in the vision, and them that sat on them, having breastplates of fire, and of jacinth, and brimstone: and the *heads* of the horses were as the heads of lions; and out of their *mouths* issued fire and smoke and brimstone.

[Rev 9:18] By these three was the third part of [the] men killed, by the fire, and by the smoke, and by the brimstone, which issued out of their *mouths*.

[Rev 9:19] For their power is in their *mouth*, and in their *tails*: for their *tails* were like unto serpents, and had *heads*, and with them they do hurt.

In order to understand what the horses look like, let us examine the Scripture carefully. According to verses 17–19, the horses have two kinds of "heads." The first kind appears in verses 17 and 18—the "heads of the horses" that have "mouths." The second kind appears in verse 19—the "heads" of "their tails." These heads are two different kinds of heads: one is the head of the horse, while the other is the head of the horse's tail.

In verse 19, the "mouth" is written in singular and "tails" plural in the original Greek text, indicating that out of one mouth are issued multiple "tails" having heads. Retranslated, verse 19 starts, "For their power is in their mouth, and in their tails [coming out of the mouth]." In other words, each tail has its own head and comes out of the mouth.

In verses 17 and 18, the words "heads" and "mouths" are associated with the "horses," all in plural form. Whether there are one or more mouths on each head of the horses is not explicitly described; there may be one or more mouths attached to each head.

Having established an understanding of the structures of the horse, let us now examine how the horses actually inflict injury and death. According to verses 17–19, there are substances that come out of the horses' mouths that inflict casualties. In other words, the structural parts of the horses themselves do not actually cause direct harm. At first glance, the Scripture seems to reveal that the fire, the smoke, and the brimstone that come out of the mouths kill the third part of the men (Rev 9:18). In addition, the "tails" that have "heads" come out of the mouths in verse 19 and hurt people.

How, then, do the tails inflict casualties? The description, "tails were like unto serpents," in verse 19 suggests the long shape of the tail and its lethality at the front where its head is. These befit the features of a missile. Verse 19 writes "tails . . . had heads, and with them they do hurt." From a grammatical perspective, it may seem unclear whether it is the tail or its head that hurts. Yet, it is suggested that the head of the tail is the part that hurts,[6] which becomes apparent by the following reasoning.

Verse 19 states that "tails . . . had heads, and with them they do hurt" people. Yet, verse 19 also states that the "power" is in the horse's "mouth" and "tails," not the "heads" of the tails. Such expressions in the Scripture indicate that the capability to hurt people is clearly distinct from the "power" in the "mouth" and "tails." In fact, this "power" (ἐξουσία, exousia) is defined as: "1. power of choice, liberty of doing as one pleases; 2. physical and mental power."[7] Such definition aids in interpreting the nature of the "mouth" and "tails," indicating that it is the "heads" that directly hurt men—that is, the "heads" of the tails in verse 19. As further discussion below shows, these parts, the mouth and the tails, have the physical or intelligent power to propel or guide missiles.

A clear understanding can be reached about the "power . . . in their tails" upon reviewing how the same words were used, "hurt" and "power," in describing the fifth trumpet, the BP Deepwater Horizon oil spill:

> [Rev 9:3] And there came out of the smoke locusts upon the earth: and unto them was given *power*, as the scorpions of the earth have *power*.

[Rev 9:4] And it was commanded them that they should not *hurt* the grass of the earth, neither any green thing, neither any tree; but only those men which have not the seal of God in their foreheads.

[Rev 9:10] And they had tails like unto scorpions, and there were stings in their tails: and their *power* was to *hurt* [the] men five months.

As interpreted in the previous chapter, the dispersant sprayed over the oil spill in the fifth trumpet hurt the men but left the grass, green things, and any tree unscathed. The "power" given to the "locusts" in verse 3 and that to their "tails"[8] in verse 10 were in the dispersant spraying aircrafts and the dispersant spraying nozzle equipment respectively. In other words, the "stings," the chemical dispersant that comes out of the tails of the locusts, could be in effect only if the "locusts" and the "tails" wielded their "power."

The power of the tails in Revelation 9:19 can be interpreted in the same manner as that of the locusts and the tails in the fifth trumpet. How the "mouth" and the "tails" wield their "power" determines how the actual hurting of people occurs. Just as the dispersant spraying nozzle opens and closes to control the emission of the chemicals when the aircraft flies to the target area, the mouth and the tails also have the power over the ejection and the flight of missiles by controlling the launching and the propulsion systems, respectively. If the impulse energy is released from the tail, the missile will be on flight; if the impulse energy is not activated, the payloads will never be delivered to the target.

Understanding the definition of the "power" perhaps requires a more advanced understanding of missiles' capability. If the missiles have a certain level of artificial intelligence that can track the target or navigate to target with homing guidance, this technology can also be the "power" in the tails. Thus, the power of the tail could include the capability of the missiles to change their flight direction as guided by its tracking radar. The power in the mouth is the impulse launching mechanism. Through the mouth, or the opening of the launch tube, the missiles are ejected.

One possible example of the "horses," SA-8 GECKO, is in Fig. 8-2. It is a mobile surface-to-air (SAM) missile system. It is equipped with radars and antennas capable of detecting and tracking the enemy. "The first production version of this system was identified as SA-8a, which only had 4 launcher rails and exposed missiles. The SA-8b typically has two BAZ-5937 resupply/transloader vehicles, carrying 18 missiles each (boxed in sets of three) that supports a battery of four TELARs [transporter erector launcher and radars]. A target can be brought under fire both with one missile as well as a volley of two missiles. This system is also air transportable."[9]

This explanation suggests that "the tail with its head" is a missile, and "the head of the tail" is the warhead that detonates or hurts. The capability to "hurt" is in the "head" of the tail, while the "power" is in the "tail." The horse may have multiple mouths, and each mouth can issue multiple "tails having heads." Again, the fact that the "mouth" is singular whereas the "tails" are plural in verse 19 suggests that a single opening can fire multiple missiles.

Then what about the fire, the smoke, and the brimstone that issue out of the horses' mouths (Rev 9:18)? The Scripture says that "By these three was the third part of men killed." Would the fire, the smoke, and the brimstone really kill the third part of men? In other words, would weapons that shoot fire, smoke, and brimstone be used in a global-scale warfare? The bombs used in the First World War were described as "hail and fire" (Rev 8:7). The atomic bomb used in the Second World War was described "as it were a great mountain burning with fire" (Rev 8:8). In the sixth trumpet, many more men will be killed than in these two world wars. Compared to fire, smoke, and brimstone, the bombs in the first two world wars are probably significantly more effective in causing casualties. Then, why does the Scripture write that these three substances killed the third part of men?

Fig. 8-2. SA-8 GECKO surface-to-air missile system.[10]

The technology in weaponry today is far more advanced than that of the twentieth century. Further understanding of the weaponry reveals that what John saw in his vision was most likely the missiles being launched and killing many. When a missile is launched, fire, smoke, and brimstone accompany the missile from the moment it is launched from the "mouth" of the "horse" until it hits its target. [11] In other words, John witnessed the entire trajectory of the missiles issued from the launching pad reaching the target areas, and eventually killing many with the warheads. In fact, John witnessed the technological advance in weaponry throughout the twentieth century and beyond—bombs in WWI as described in the first trumpet, an atomic bomb in WWII as in the second trumpet, and missiles possibly with nuclear warheads in WWIII as in the sixth trumpet.

The process of missile attack precisely matches the order in which the hurting and killing are described in the Scripture regarding WWIII of the sixth trumpet. In verse 17, the three substances—the fire, the smoke, and the brimstone—that are issued at the launch of missiles are introduced. Verse 18 explains the fact that these substances accompany the missile during the entire trajectory, from launch to detonation. Verse 19 further explains how the missiles' trajectory "were like unto serpents" during the entire trajectory, then precisely describes that it is the warheads of the missiles—the "heads"—that hurt and kill upon detonation.

Why does the description "were like unto serpents" appear in verse 19, but not in previous verses? John wrote in the order he witnessed the entire missile attack—first the launch in verse 17; then the fire, smoke, and brimstone that accompany the missile from launch to the target in verses 17 and 18; then the snake-like trajectory in verse 19; then the detonation upon reaching the target in verse 19.

Based on the interpretation so far, the "horses" in the sixth trumpet cannot be tanks, as they do not fire missiles. Furthermore, if the "horses" in the sixth trumpet refer to conventional weaponry only, it would take a long time to kill an immense number of people. At such rate, killing the third part of the world population may be nearly impossible. In contrast, latest technology allows weapons of mass destruction (WMD), such as nuclear bombs, to be attached as warheads to missiles that can target larger crowds, rendering the fulfillment of the WWIII prophecy of the sixth trumpet possible. What John witnessed in the vision was most likely missiles with nuclear warheads killing a third of the world population.

If such nuclear applications are the weapons described in the said passage, astronomical casualties would be a natural consequence. In turn, the war's duration may also be reduced significantly by the use of nuclear weaponry. If only conventional weapons are used, the duration of the war in the sixth trumpet would be prolonged for the prophesied casualties to be reached.

The Location and the Duration

In a previous section, the global scale of World War III was discussed. When and where, then, would World War III occur? Remember that the trumpets have decadal intervals. The third, the fourth, and the fifth trumpets occurred in 1986, in c. 2000, and in 2010, respectively. The intervals between these trumpet events decreased with each trumpet. This trend is observed throughout the trumpet series, except between the second and the third trumpets, as shown in Fig. 8-1. Assuming this trend holds, one may expect when the sixth trumpet event may take place.

[Rev 9:14] Saying to the sixth angel which had the trumpet, Loose the four angels which are bound in the great *river Euphrates.*

This verse provides an absolute clue that the war will revolve around the Euphrates River. The Euphrates flows through Turkey, Syria, and Iraq. Note that currently, in July 2018, the war with Islamic State is not completely finished in the area. At this point, let us review how World War II was prophesied:

[Rev 8:8] And the second angel sounded, and as it were a great mountain burning with fire was cast into the sea: and the third part of the sea became blood;

What is noteworthy from the WWII description in Revelation 8:8 is that only the nuclear bombing in Japan was portrayed. But in reality, there was a series of long battles throughout the war's duration, including Hitler's Holocaust against the Jews. But the Bible excluded the majority of them and limited the prophetic description to one of the most characteristic incidents of the war, an incident unprecedented in the world: "as it were a great mountain burning with fire was cast into the sea."

Likewise, it can be speculated that WWIII may not be limited to the Euphrates River area. While the river runs through Turkey, Syria, and Iraq, the war will ultimately involve many nations, drawing many young men to a death march.

What about the duration of the war? As previously discussed, the advance in weaponry, such as the use of nuclear missiles, will shorten the duration of the war.

> [Rev 9:15] And the four angels were loosed, which were prepared *for* (εἰς, *eis*) *an hour, and a day, and a month, and a year* (τὴν ὥραν καὶ ἡμέραν καὶ μῆνα καὶ ἐνιαυτόν, *tēn hōran kai hēmeran kai mēna kai eniauton*), for to slay the third part of [the] men.

The word-for-word translation of the italicized phrase above in English becomes: "for *the* hour and a day and a month and a year." In other words, in Greek, there is "the" in front of "hour" only, not in front of "day," "month," or "year." The interpretations thereof have two streams. The first standpoint is explained through an excerpt from Albert Barnes' *Notes on the Bible*:

> The Greek—εἰς(eis)—means properly "unto, with reference to"; and the sense is, that, with reference to that hour, they had all the requisite preparation. Prof. Stuart explains it as meaning that they were "prepared for the particular year, month, day, and hour, destined

by God for the great catastrophe which is to follow." The meaning, however, rather seems to be that they were prepared, not for the commencement of such a period, but they were prepared for the whole period indicated by the hour, the day, the month, and the year; that is, that the continuance of this "woe" would extend along through the whole period. For:

(a) this is the natural interpretation of the word "for" — εἰς (eis);

(b) it makes the whole sentence intelligible—for though it might be proper to say of anything that it was "prepared for an hour," indicating the commencement of what was to be done, it is not usual to say of anything that it is "prepared for an hour, a month, a day, a year," when the design is merely to indicate the beginning of it; and,

(c) it is in accordance with the prediction respecting the first "woe" Rev 9:5, where the time is specified in language similar to this, to wit, "five months." It seems to me, therefore, that we are to regard the time here mentioned as a prophetic indication of the period during which this woe would continue.[12]

According to this view, the war duration amounts to a total of one year, one month, one day, and one hour—in other words, thirteen months and one day and one hour—which corresponds to a little more than a year. However, reading how the five months' duration of the fifth trumpet was prophesied in the original Greek suggests otherwise:

[Rev 9:5] And to them it was given that they should not kill them, but that *they should be tormented five months* (βασανισθῶσιν μῆνας πέντε; *basanisthōsin mēnas pente*): and their torment was as the torment of a scorpion, when he striketh a man.

In this verse, there is no preposition "εἰς" (*eis;* unto, with reference to) used in designating the five months. Therefore, the insertion of "εἰς" (*eis*) in Revelation 9:15 is suggestive of a different view than the duration, contrary to Barnes' interpretation. This leads to examination of the second standpoint, represented in *Vincent's Word Studies*:

> For an hour and a day and a month and a year—This rendering is wrong, since it conveys the idea that the four periods mentioned are to be combined as representing the length of the preparation or of the continuance of the plague. But it is to be noted that neither the article nor the preposition are repeated before *day* and *month* and *year*. The meaning is that the angels are prepared unto the *hour* appointed by God, and that this hour shall fall in its appointed day and month and year.[13]

According to the grammatical approach, this second interpretation can also be convincing. If the death toll from WWIII will surpass those of WWI and WWII, it may be rather difficult for such many people to be killed during thirteen months' duration.

The proponents of the first interpretation may insist that the possible use of nuclear bombs can account for the large number of deaths in about a year's length. However, the Bible does not explicitly indicate that deaths would be caused by nuclear meltdown only. The Scripture clearly says that the third part of men are said to be killed. The Scripture also makes it clear that two hundred million soldiers fight in the war. The fact that such significant number of horsemen participate in the war perhaps shows that WWIII may not be an outright nuclear war only. After all, if the war was an all-out nuclear war, then only the operators to control the nuclear missiles would be needed.

> [Rev 9:17] And thus I saw the horses in the vision, and *them that sat on them*, having breastplates of fire, and of jacinth, and brimstone: and the heads of the horses were as the heads of lions; and out of their mouths issued fire and smoke and brimstone.

The fact that John mentions "them that sat on [the horses]" suggests that the war is most likely going to be fought using human-controlled weapons. As the current advancement in technology is gearing towards the use of drones and automatic patrolling robots, the future armament will not involve many humans actually fighting in the battlefields.

However, John describes "them" that are physically sitting on the horses, and they cannot be of robotic entities that control the man-made horses. Designing a drone is one thing, and developing a man-shaped robot to control the drone, vehicles, and such armament is another. Therefore, John's descriptions here seem to support that WWIII will be carried out mostly using weapons that are controlled by humans, and further suggest that WWIII will occur before the full development and application stage of such advanced robotics and artificial intelligence arrives.

The war fought with conventional weapons may prolong the war significantly in length, compared to an all-out nuclear war. For instance, the war in Syria that started in the spring of 2011 has led to over 220,000 fatalities over a span of four years.[14] This death toll corresponds to about 1 percent of the Syrian population.

In the case of WWII, about 3 percent of world population then (66 million fatalities out of 2.3 billion) lost lives throughout the six years of warfare. In other words, the wars fought with conventional weapons can ravage only a small percentage of the entire world population. In the Syrian Civil War also, only a small portion of the population was killed as most of the combats were conducted by conventional weapons. But the Bible warns there will be the third part of men slain in WWIII of the sixth trumpet.

The current lethal weapons are far advanced in precision and firepower when compared with the ones used in WWII. Conceivably, killing 3 percent of mankind in modern day using the upgraded conventional weapons would take much less time than in WWII. However, killing a third of either the entire world population (2.5 billion) or the population in the participating nations could still take up significant length of time.

Therefore, if WWIII is fought with conventional weapons, the war may prolong for quite a long time. However, if the war is to end rather abruptly sooner with a large number of deaths incurred, then the use of nuclear weapons may be anticipated. In other words, if a combination of nuclear and conventional weapons is used in WWIII, the proportion of nuclear weapons used will determine how short the duration of WWIII would be.

If the first interpretation, that the duration of the war is thirteen months and one day and one hour, is correct, then the sixth trumpet may be initiated in a way that conventional weapons are used initially, and then nuclear missiles are used for most of the duration of thirteen months and one day and one hour. If the second interpretation, that the four angels in Revelation 9:15 are loosed in the appointed hour on the appointed day and month and year, is correct, then there would be a specific hour on an appointed date that the Third World War will clearly begin.

Regardless of which one of the two interpretations on the expression "for *the* hour and a day and a month and a year" is correct, one certain thing is that the beginning point of the war may be apparent. If the expression is interpreted to be the "duration," then it would mean that the start and the end of the war would be unequivocal. If the angels prepared for slaying the third part of the men are loosed at that "precise time," then the war's specific outbreak time would also be unequivocal. Consequently, either interpretation will lead to the same conclusion—a clear starting time for WWIII.

Such conclusion is based on a premise that the loosing of the four angels in the Euphrates is a spiritual event that will also substantiate into a physical incident at the same time. The current situation in Syria and Iraq will most likely escalate into a global war, regardless of the outcome of the war with Islamic State. In July 2018, time is ticking toward the sounding of the sixth trumpet, and the current situation is most likely the prelude to WWIII.

Countries Involved in WWIII

Let us now examine the following verse again, focusing on the riders that sat on the horses:

> [Rev 9:17] And thus I saw the horses in the vision, and them that sat on them, having *breastplates of fire, and of jacinth, and brimstone* (θώρακας πυρίνους καὶ ὑακινθίνους καὶ θειώδεις, *thōrakas purinous kai hyakinthinous kai theiōdeis*): and the heads of the horses were as the heads of lions; and out of their mouths issued fire and smoke and brimstone.

The riders have breastplates of three different colors—fire, jacinth, and brimstone. The "fire" is red, and "brimstone" yellow. What about "jacinth?" According to *Vincent's Word Studies*, the noun "jacinth" is "the name of a flower and also of a precious stone . . . As a stone, it is identified by some with the sapphire. As to color, the hyacinth of the Greeks seems to have comprehended the iris, gladiolus, and larkspur. Hence the different accounts of its color in classical writings, varying from red to black. A dull, dark blue seems to be meant here."[15]

According to Albert Barnes' *Notes on the Bible*, "the color denoted is that of the hyacinth—a flower of a deep purple or reddish blue."[16] Other commentaries say this is simply a hyacinth color, which in ancient time represented the dark blue iris.[17] *John Gill's Exposition of the Entire Bible* also writes it as sky colour.[18] Overall, scholars concur that the jacinth or hyacinth represents a blue color.

Breastplates of fire, jacinth, and brimstone (θώρακας πυρίνους καὶ ὑακινθίνους καὶ θειώδεις, *thōrakas purinous kai hyakinthinous kai theiōdeis*) are mentioned in the verse of interest. The first step to understanding what the breastplates look like would be to figure out whether they are three different kinds of breastplates or three colors comprising a single breastplate. However, the grammar of the text does not provide a clear-cut answer. Therefore, both arguments exist: some argue there are a breastplate of red, a breastplate of blue, and another of yellow, while others interpret that there are all three colors used on the same breastplate.[19]

If the constituents of the breastplates are referring to the colors, what would be the significance of the colors? In a war, colors are part of what identifies the army or nation participating in the war, as colors are incorporated into the designs of flags, armor, and weaponry. Thus, the search for a breastplate painted with three colors of red, blue, and yellow was done, but was unsuccessful. A weapon painted with the three colors was practically non-existent. In addition, most of the superpowers and Middle Eastern nations do not have flags that use the three colors.

In fact, it is unlikely for a single nation to employ all three colors mentioned in the prophecy, as the war will be fought by more than one nation. For this reason, the prophecy most likely describes breastplates of different colors symbolizing different groups of nations.

If the war of the sixth trumpet is indeed a world war, the three colors would most likely represent as many participating nations as possible. Rather than symbolizing a particular country, a specific color could represent the coalition among a number of nations or a characteristic of a region.

Historically, different regions of the world have been represented by certain colors. Prior to 1951, the official Olympic Charter stated that the five colored rings of the Olympic symbol together represent the union of different continents: "blue for Europe, yellow for Asia, black for Africa, green for Australia and red for America." However, in later years, the International Olympic Committee (IOC) removed the original clause that associated colors with respective continents, stating that "no definite proof can be found that this allocation of colours was P. de Coubertin's original idea at the very most he might perhaps have admitted it afterwards."[20]

The symbolism from the Olympics may render a new interpretation of the colors of the breastplates.[21] The three colors in Revelation 9:17 may suggest that the nations from the Americas, Europe and Asia will participate in the Third World War. Since the colors are on the breastplates of those sitting on the horses, the description may be representing the deployment of missile systems from those countries. However, the verse in question does not limit the participating nations to three continents only, for the nations from Africa and Australia (and Oceania) could also fight in World War III, but perhaps without a large number of missile systems or other heavy military equipment involvement.

Why Does God Allow WWIII?

The Scripture describes the people who survived WWIII of the sixth trumpet as follows:

> [Rev 9:20] And the rest of the men which were not killed by these plagues *yet repented not* of the works of their hands, that they should not worship devils, and

idols of gold, and silver, and brass, and stone, and of wood: which neither can see, nor hear, nor walk:
[Rev 9:21] Neither repented they of their murders, nor of their sorceries, nor of their fornication, nor of their thefts.

Even after suffering much through WWIII, people do not realize the reason why God allowed such an affliction. In verse 20, they "yet repented not" of their idolatry. In other words, God, through such an enormous catastrophic period, wants people to repent of their sins, but people are not too concerned about His intent.

But what God has purposed and uttered will be done according to His will, and His word will bear fruit.

[Isa 55:11] So shall my word be that goeth forth out of my mouth: it shall not return unto me void, but it shall accomplish that which I please, and it shall prosper in the thing whereto I sent it.

There will be some people who will listen to the word of God and repent of their sins during the harsh time of WWIII. During the time of peace, people pursue worldly things, and they are not much interested in the word of God. But during the war, many of them have a sole interest in knowing how to survive. They will be humble or be humbled in many ways, and will listen to the Good News of God.

For many non-Christians and weak Christians, WWIII will be a time to ponder on the existential problems: "Who am I? What is the purpose of my life? Why am I here? What will happen to me tomorrow? Can I survive?" They most likely would not have had much time to ask themselves these questions before the war, as their minds were busy, attached to the things in this world.

Therefore, to the ones with humble hearts, God will send His messengers to share the gospel. It will truly be a "golden time" for Christians to obey the Lord to go, baptize, and teach people to observe God's word.

> [Mt 28:19] *Go* ye therefore, and teach all nations, *baptizing* them in the name of the Father, and of the Son, and of the Holy Ghost:
> [Mt 28:20] *Teaching* them to observe all things whatsoever I have commanded you: and, lo, I am with you alway, even unto the end of the world. Amen.

Through the book series, it became apparent that all the seals had already been opened, and the first five trumpets have also been sounded. The sixth trumpet will be sounded next, perhaps not in a distant future from July 2018.

So, what should the Christians do at this present pre-WWIII time? As discussed previously, WWIII will be a good time for Christians to share the gospel. Therefore, Christians need to learn and exercise how to use the word of God—reading, meditating, reciting, sharing, and preaching.

> [1Pe 3:15] But sanctify the Lord God in your hearts: and *be ready always to give an answer to every man that asketh you* a reason of the hope that is in you with meekness and fear:

The Lord commanded us to pray for the laborers.

> [Lk 10:2] Therefore said he unto them, *The harvest truly is great, but the labourers are few*: pray ye therefore the Lord of the harvest, that he would send forth labourers into his harvest.

The Third World War will truly be a time of harvest, yet to Him, "the laborers are few." In other words, the Lord wants to raise more laborers and send them to the field, especially in the time of harvest.

> [2Ti 2:19] Nevertheless the foundation of God standeth sure, having this seal, *The Lord knoweth them that are his.* And, Let every one that nameth the name of Christ depart from iniquity.
> [2Ti 2:20] But in a great house there are not only vessels of gold and of silver, but also of wood and of earth; and some to honour, and some to dishonour.
> [2Ti 2:21] If a man therefore purge himself from these, he shall be a vessel unto honour, sanctified, and *meet for the master's use,* and *prepared* unto every good work.

The Lord knows His people, especially the laborers. If a man is prepared, he will be known by the Lord, and will be used by the Master.

Now, what about survival? During WWIII, the third part of the world population will be killed. Will you be among the third part, or will you be among the surviving two thirds? If you are a man of God, and if you really want to serve the Lord, it would be best not to become too concerned about your survival. After all, the Lord commanded His disciples to follow Him, even not to concern their lives, but to concentrate on obeying the Lord.

> [Lk 14:26] If any man come to me, and hate not his father, and mother, and wife, and children, and brethren, and sisters, yea, and his own *life* also, he cannot be my disciple.

This completes the interpretation on the first part of the sixth trumpet. The second part of the sixth trumpet in Revelation 10 is interpreted in the next chapter. The last part of the sixth trumpet, the two witnesses, will be discussed in the next volume, as it is related to the rapture.

CHAPTER 9.
THE SIXTH TRUMPET:
A LITTLE BOOK
AND THE SEVEN THUNDERS

As discussed previously, the sixth trumpet, the second "woe," starts when the sixth angel sounds his trumpet in Revelation 9:13. The sixth trumpet is declared completed when the Scripture writes "The second woe has passed" in Revelation 11:14. Therefore, the sixth trumpet includes World War III in Revelation 9:13–21, the uttering of the seven thunders and John's eating of a little book in Revelation chapter 10, and the two witnesses' prophesying in Revelation 11:3–13.

The sixth trumpet does not end in chapter 9, where the first part of the sixth trumpet is written about, and continues unto chapter 11, where the seventh trumpet is prophesied. The entire chapter 10 of Revelation is dedicated to a little book and the seven thunders, the topics which may seem to be appearing out of nowhere. However, chapter 10 actually describes an important event that takes part in the middle of sixth trumpet, between WWIII in chapter 9 and the testimony of the two witnesses in chapter 11. The chapter reads:

> [Rev 10:1] And I saw another mighty angel come down from heaven, clothed with a cloud: and a

rainbow was upon his head, and his face was as it were the sun, and his feet as pillars of fire:

[Rev 10:2] And he had in his hand *a little book* open: and he set his right foot upon the sea, and his left foot on the earth,

[Rev 10:3] And cried with a loud voice, as when a lion roareth: and when he had cried, *seven thunders uttered* their voices.

[Rev 10:4] And when the *seven thunders had uttered* their voices, I was about to write: and I heard a voice from heaven saying unto me, Seal up those things which the *seven thunders uttered*, and write them not.

[Rev 10:5] And the angel which I saw stand upon the sea and upon the earth lifted up his hand to heaven,

[Rev 10:6] And sware by him that liveth for ever and ever, who created heaven, and the things that therein are, and the earth, and the things that therein are, and the sea, and the things which are therein, that there should be time no longer:

[Rev 10:7] But in the days of the voice of the seventh angel, when he shall begin to sound, the mystery of God should be finished, as he hath declared to his servants the prophets.

[Rev 10:8] And the voice which I heard from heaven spake unto me again, and said, Go and take the *little book* which is open in the hand of the angel which standeth upon the sea and upon the earth.

[Rev 10:9] And I went unto the angel, and said unto him, Give me the *little book*. And he said unto me, Take it, and eat it up; and it shall make thy belly bitter, but it shall be in thy mouth sweet as honey.

[Rev 10:10] And I took the *little book* out of the angel's hand, and ate it up; and it was in my mouth sweet as

honey: and as soon as I had eaten it, my belly was bitter.
[Rev 10:11] And he said unto me, Thou must prophesy again before many peoples, and nations, and tongues, and kings.

As will be discussed in detail later, this chapter is relevant to the Bible prophecy about seventy weeks that appear in Daniel 9:24–27, perhaps the most important prophecy about apocalypse. Lord Jesus had also referred to the book of Daniel, especially about the abomination of desolation:

[Mt 24:15] When ye therefore shall see the *abomination of desolation*, spoken of by Daniel the prophet, stand in the holy place, (whoso readeth, let him understand:)
[Mk 13:14] But when ye shall see the *abomination of desolation*, spoken of by Daniel the prophet, standing where it ought not, (let him that readeth understand,) then let them that be in Judaea flee to the mountains:

In the Old Testament, prophecies about the "last days," "latter days," and "the day of the Lord" hold significant positions and are referred to as "the day of Christ," or "the day of the Lord" in the New Testament. The prophecies point that the Antichrist will manifest in the final seven years, the period referred to as the "last week" of the seventy weeks in the book of Daniel:

[Da 9:27] And he [the Antichrist-to-be] shall confirm the *covenant with many for one week*: and in the *midst of the week* he shall cause the sacrifice and the oblation to cease, and for the overspreading of abominations he shall make it desolate, even until the consummation, and that determined shall be poured upon the desolate.

In this passage, the word "week" is "literally, sevened, i.e. a week (specifically, of years):—seven, week."[1] Therefore, one week here means seven years.[2, 3] Also, the final seven years divide into two halves, each with forty-two months, or 3.5 years. In the middle of the final seven-year period, the Antichrist, or the beast, shall enter the temple and call himself god, and the false prophet will force everybody to worship the image of the beast.

> [2Th 2:4] Who [the Antichrist] opposeth and exalteth himself above all that is called God, or that is worshipped; so that he as God sitteth in the temple of God, *shewing himself that he is God.*
> [Rev 13:15] And he [the false prophet] had power to give life unto the image of the beast, that the image of the beast should both speak, and *cause that as many as would not worship the image of the beast should be killed.*

The prophecy on the final seven years is truly weighty in every aspect—the timeline of the last days, the abundant descriptions on events to happen before and after, and the appearance of the Antichrist.

Therefore, it is only natural to expect the prophetic descriptions on the "final week" to appear in the New Testament, especially in the book of Revelation, which is full of apocalyptic events. The event that marks the beginning of the final week, the Antichrist-to-be making the covenant with many, would be no exception. However, many find it difficult to locate the covenant confirmed for one week in Daniel 9:27, the Seven-Year Treaty, in the book of Revelation. At first glance, the Seven-Year Treaty in Daniel does not seem to appear in Revelation.

Could such crucial prophecy on the Antichrist-to-be confirming a covenant with many that would mark the beginning of Daniel's final week be omitted in Revelation? To solve the quandary, let us ponder upon the following pivotal hints.

Where is the Seven-Year Treaty Described?

According to the interpretations so far, the first trumpet was the First World War, the second trumpet WWII, the third trumpet the Chernobyl Nuclear Plant accident, the fourth trumpet the Global Dimming phenomenon, the fifth trumpet the BP Deepwater Horizon oil spill in the Gulf of Mexico, and the first part of the sixth trumpet WWIII.

If Revelation is read with the sound assumption that it is written sequentially and in chronological order, then one can readily discover that the sixth trumpet begins in chapter 9 and does not end until chapter 11, and that the seventh trumpet sounds in chapter 11 after the sixth trumpet, the second woe, has finished.

> [Rev 11:14] *The second woe [the sixth trumpet] is past;* and, behold, the third woe cometh quickly.
> [Rev 11:15] And the seventh angel sounded; and there were great voices in heaven, saying, The kingdoms of this world are become the kingdoms of our Lord, and of his Christ; and he shall reign for ever and ever.

If Revelation chapter 10 is relevant to the Seven-Year Treaty, then the order of the events written in Revelation would be indicating that the fifth trumpet and World War III of the sixth trumpet in chapter 9 will happen prior to the Seven-Year Treaty, and the seventh trumpet in chapter 11 will happen after the confirmation of the Seven-Year Treaty.

Before discussing details on Revelation chapters 11 to 13, let us first compare the time-related expressions in Daniel and Revelation. The following are verses in Daniel concerning the final week's timeline and determined hours:

[Da 7:25] And he [the Antichrist] shall speak great words against the most High, and shall wear out the saints of the most High, and think to change times and laws: and they shall be given into his hand until *a time and times and the dividing of time.*

[Da 9:27] And he [the Antichrist] shall confirm the *covenant with many for one week*: and in *the midst of the week* he shall cause the sacrifice and the oblation to cease, and for the overspreading of abominations he shall make it desolate, even until the consummation, and that determined shall be poured upon the desolate.

[Da 12:7] And I heard the man clothed in linen, which was upon the waters of the river, when he held up his right hand and his left hand unto heaven, and sware by him that liveth for ever that it shall be for *a time, times, and an half*; and when he shall have accomplished to scatter the power of the holy people, all these things shall be finished.

[Da 12:11] And from the time that the daily sacrifice shall be taken away, and the abomination that maketh desolate set up, there shall be *a thousand two hundred and ninety days.*

In the above verses, "a time and times and the dividing of time" or "a time, times, and an half" corresponds to 3.5 years or forty-two months, the second half of the final seven-year period. The expression "a thousand two hundred and ninety days" is related to 1,260 days. A total of 1,290 days includes 30 days in addition to 1,260 days which is equal to 3.5 years. The additional 30 days will be discussed in the next volume of the series.

If Revelation chapter 10 describes the confirmation of the covenant that would mark the beginning of the final week mentioned in Daniel, then there should be clues in Revelation for readers to recognize the covenant. Starting from Revelation 11, concrete numbers are provided to indicate points in the timeline. What were referred in Daniel as "a time, times, and an half" regarding the "final week" are expressed as "forty and two months," "1,260 days," and "a time, and times, and half a time" to denote the same length of time in the book of Revelation:

> [Rev 11:2] But the court which is without the temple leave out, and measure it not; for it is given unto the Gentiles: and the holy city shall they tread under foot *forty and two months*.
> [Rev 11:3] And I will give power unto my two witnesses, and they shall prophesy *a thousand two hundred and threescore days*, clothed in sackcloth.
> [Rev 12:6] And the woman fled into the wilderness, where she hath a place prepared of God, that they should feed her there *a thousand two hundred and threescore days*.
> [Rev 12:14] And to the woman were given two wings of a great eagle, that she might fly into the wilderness, into her place, where she is nourished for *a time, and times, and half a time*, from the face of the serpent.
> [Rev 13:5] And there was given unto him a mouth speaking great things and blasphemies; and power was given unto him to continue *forty and two months*.

What is noteworthy is that there are no such time-related expressions or numbers related to Daniel's prophecy appearing before chapter 11 in Revelation. Before chapter 11, there are no expressions like "forty and two months," "1,260 days," or "a time, and times, and half a time."

As these time-related expressions and numbers in the book of Daniel describe the final seven-year period, the presence of corresponding expressions and numbers in Revelation chapter 11 reveals that the chapter is pertinent to the final seven years. The facts that Revelation chapters 1 to 9 have no allusion to the "final week" and that events in chapter 11 are pertinent to the final seven years strongly suggest that Revelation chapter 10 writes of the Seven-Year Treaty that marks the beginning of the "final week." In fact, more evidence that chapter 10 is about the Seven-Year Treaty can be found in Revelation chapters 11 through 13.

First, Revelation 11:2 mentions "forty and two months" period during which the Gentiles tread the holy city under foot, and chapter 12 describes the 3.5 years' period of Dragon's great persecution of the saints. These two periods are actually the same period, the latter half of the final seven-year period, and are expressed as "a thousand two hundred and threescore days" in Revelation 12:6 and "a time, and times, and half a time" in Revelation 12:14. Examining the Scripture reveals that this period corresponds to Daniel's "a time and times and the dividing of time," the period when the saints are persecuted (Da 7:25) and the time of Jacob's trouble (Jer 30:7). The details of Revelation 12 will be discussed thoroughly in Volumes 3 and 4.

> [Jer 30:7] Alas! for that day is great, so that none is like it: it is even the *time of Jacob's trouble*; but he shall be saved out of it.

According to Daniel, the persecution of the saints in the final seven-year period occurs during the latter 3.5 years (Da 7:25). Revelation 12 describes such persecution, and thus, indicates the first 3.5 years must have been described before Chapter 12 in Revelation.

Second, in Revelation 13:7–18, the Antichrist and the false prophet start making war with the saints and overcome them and begin to force all people, small and great, rich and poor, to receive the mark of the beast on the right hand or on their foreheads and to worship the image of the beast. If the false prophet were to begin enforcing the mark of the beast and persecuting those who refuse from the very middle of the final seven-year period as Daniel 9:27 prophesies, then it suffices to conclude that the chapter 13 also contains prophecies on the latter half of the seven-year period, like chapter 12.

Third, as long as the assumption that the book of Revelation is written sequentially and in chronological order is not violated, one will recognize that the 1,260 days (3.5 years) of the two witnesses' testimony in Chapter 11 is the first half of the seven-year period.

> [Rev 11:3] And I will give power unto my two witnesses, and they shall prophesy *a thousand two hundred and threescore days*, clothed in sackcloth.

This particular period described in the passage above is characterized by absence of persecution of the saints. As persecution is related to the latter 3.5 years of the final seven-year period, it can be deduced that Revelation 11:3 describes the first 3.5 years of the final seven-year period. The details of Revelation 11 will be discussed in Volume 3.

Then, when does the seven-year period begin? It must begin with the Seven-Year Treaty, as prophesied in Daniel 9:27. At the midpoint of the seven-year period, the Antichrist begins persecution against the saints. Three and a half years prior to the midpoint is the beginning of the seven-year period, clearly marked by the confirmation of the Seven-Year Treaty.

As mentioned before, Revelation chapters 1 to 9 do not mention the time-related expressions similar to those in Daniel. They are first introduced in Revelation 11, in which the first half of the seven-year period with regard to the two witnesses and the second half with regard to the Gentiles' treading the holy city are described. The Seven-Year Treaty signals the beginning of the final seven years of mankind before the millennial kingdom, and should be placed after chapter 9 and before chapter 11, hence chapter 10. Needless to say, examining and understanding Revelation chapter 10 is crucial.

The Mighty Angel

Revelation chapter 10 starts with a mighty angel coming down from heaven.

> [Rev 10:1] And I saw *another mighty angel* come down from heaven, clothed with a cloud: and a rainbow was upon his head, and his face was as it were the sun, and his feet as pillars of fire:

Who is this angel? The mighty angel has specific descriptions, "cloud," "rainbow," "sun," and "pillars of fire" in verse 1 that allude to the characteristics of the chapter. Some state that the magnificence of the cloud, rainbow, sun, and pillars of fire resembles those used to describe Jesus in Revelation 1:13–16, and argue that the mighty angel in question refers to "God" or "Christ."[4, 5]

However, such argument is not definitive, as Revelation never refers to the Lord as an angel. Besides, even if Jesus could ever be described as an "angel," Jesus certainly would not be described as "another angel" (Rev 10:1) as opposed to simply an "angel." If Jesus were "another mighty angel," then it would suggest that at least one more "mighty angel" exists, whose might or power is comparable to or rivals Jesus. But such angels do not exist. Therefore, the interpretation of "another mighty angel" as God or Jesus cannot be correct.

Another school of thought exists, that the mighty angel is the angel "Gabriel." This speculation is founded on the etymological inference that the Greek word "mighty" (ἰσχυρός, *ischyros*) corresponds to a Hebrew word גֶּבֶר (*geber*), of which three-letter consonants are the same as the first three consonants of the name of the angel Gabriel mentioned in the book of Daniel.[6] The following evidence in addition to the apparent link of Gabriel's name with the Hebrew word גֶּבֶר (*geber*) solidifies that the angel in question is indeed Gabriel.

The word Gabriel (גַּבְרִיאֵל, *Gabriy'el*) is a compound word of גֶּבֶר (*geber*) meaning "a valiant man or warrior" and אֵל (*el*) meaning "the Almighty, God (god)." Hence, Gabriel signifies "warrior of God" or "man of God."[7] God sends the angel Gabriel as a messenger for very important messages. He had appeared to Daniel, Zacharias, and Mary before.

The words that Gabriel delivered in the Bible will be accomplished as they were told. As important his task is, Gabriel's rank as a mighty angel must be very high. If the mighty angel in Revelation chapter 10 is indeed Gabriel, his high rank is suggested by the descriptive words like cloud, rainbow, sun, and pillars of fire in Revelation 10:1.

> [Da 9:21] Yea, whiles I was speaking in prayer, even the man *Gabriel*, whom I had seen in the vision at the beginning, being caused to fly swiftly, touched me about the time of the evening oblation.
>
> [Da 9:22] And he informed me, and talked with me, and said, O Daniel, I am now come forth to give thee skill and understanding.
>
> [Da 9:23] At the beginning of thy supplications the commandment came forth, and I am come to shew thee; for thou art greatly beloved: therefore understand the matter, and consider the vision.
>
> [Da 9:24] *Seventy weeks are determined* upon thy people and upon thy holy city, to finish the transgression, and to make an end of sins, and to make reconciliation for iniquity, and to bring in everlasting righteousness, and to seal up the vision and prophecy, and to anoint the most Holy.

As seen in the passage above, the angel that was sent by God to notify of the seventy weeks determined upon Israelites and Jerusalem was Gabriel. Therefore, it is not farfetched to deduce that it was Gabriel again who came to prophesy regarding the "final week" in Revelation chapter 10 that would complete Daniel's seventy weeks. In fact, the coming down of Gabriel to announce the impending last week of the very seventy weeks that he had delivered vision of in Daniel chapter 9 would serve as another evidence that Revelation chapter 10 writes about the Seven-Year Treaty.

If the purpose of the mighty angel's appearance in Revelation chapter 10 is to announce the fulfillment of the last week of Daniel's seventy weeks, what is the significance of the "cloud," "rainbow," "sun," and "pillars of fire?" How do these characteristics relate to the Seven-Year Treaty?

A "rainbow" is a token of the everlasting covenant that God made with all living creatures after the flood of Noah.

[Ge 9:12] And God said, This is the *token of the covenant* which I make between me and you and every living creature that is with you, for perpetual generations:
[Ge 9:13] I do set my *bow* in the cloud, and it shall be for a *token of a covenant* between me and the earth.
[Ge 9:14] And it shall come to pass, when I bring a cloud over the earth, that the *bow* shall be seen in the cloud:
[Ge 9:15] And I will remember my *covenant*, which is between me and you and every living creature of all flesh; and the waters shall no more become a flood to destroy all flesh.
[Ge 9:16] And the *bow* shall be in the cloud; and I will look upon it, that I may remember the everlasting *covenant* between God and every living creature of all flesh that is upon the earth.

As can be seen in the passage above, the "rainbow" serves as a token and a reminder of the covenant that God made with all living creatures. In verses 15 and 16, God promised that the "rainbow" will remind Him of the everlasting covenant that "the waters shall no more become a flood to destroy all flesh."

What about the "rainbow" in Revelation chapter 10? Would it be referring to the covenant from the time of Noah? It would be very unlikely. Verse 13 in the passage above indicates that a "rainbow" is generally "a token of a covenant between me and the earth" as set by God. As angel Gabriel had delivered the promise of the seventy weeks in Daniel chapter 9, the rainbow in Revelation chapter 10 would most likely serve as a reminder of the promise from Daniel chapter 9, particularly the final seventieth week.

As discussed in Chapter 1 of this volume, all Israel is to be saved when the number of Gentile believers is filled. The world will be in its last days when this happens, as Romans 11:25–26 and Matthew 24:14 indicate. During the latter 3.5 years of the last, or the seventieth, week of the seventy weeks promised in Daniel chapter 9, persecution of the saints by the Antichrist and the consummation occur as prophesied in Daniel 9:27.

> [Da 9:27] And he shall confirm the covenant with many for one week: and in the *midst* of the week he shall cause the sacrifice and the oblation to cease, and for the overspreading of abominations he shall make it desolate, even until the *consummation*, and that determined shall be poured upon the desolate.

The latter half of the last week in Daniel chapter 9 leads to "the consummation," the last day of mankind before the millennial kingdom. During this period, the "blindness" to the truth will be removed from the Jews (Ro 11:25–26), when the gospel has reached all nations in the world (Mt 24:14). As this period is imminent, the mighty angel in Revelation chapter 10 comes down from heaven with a rainbow upon his head as God remembers His promise in Daniel chapter 9. God is faithful; He remembers and keeps His promise.

If the "rainbow" in Revelation chapter 10 is a reminder of the final seventieth week, what do the "cloud," "sun," and "pillars of fire" signify? The following verses show that God uses the cloud and fire to guide His people:

> [Ex 13:21] And the LORD went before them by day in a pillar of a *cloud*, to lead them the way; and by night in a *pillar of fire*, to give them light; to go by day and night:
> [Ex 40:38] For the *cloud* of the LORD was upon the tabernacle by day, and *fire* was on it by night, in the sight of all the house of Israel, throughout all their journeys.

The following verses show that the sun represents God and His grace and glory:

> [Ps 84:11] For the LORD God is a *sun* and shield: the LORD will give grace and glory: no good thing will he withhold from them that walk uprightly.
> [Rev 21:23] And the city had no need of the *sun*, neither of the moon, to shine in it: for the glory of God did lighten it, and the Lamb is the light thereof.

The characteristics of the mighty angel in Revelation 10:1 suggest that God remembers His promise from Daniel chapter 9 and sends the same angel, Gabriel, to deliver once again and fulfill the prophecy on the final seventieth week. Ultimately, God reminds those He loves and warns them of the imminence of the final week, and thus guides His people into the grace and the glory of the Lord Jesus Christ.

A Little Book

Through Revelation chapter 10, God announces the impending final seven-year period. As the period is the last seven years of mankind before the return of Lord Jesus Christ, God proclaims its imminence as clearly, emphatically, loudly, vividly, and explicitly as possible, with the intention to make it difficult for the readers to miss it. The focus of the chapter is on the "little book" the mighty angel has in his hand, which is most likely related to the announcement. What, then, is the "little book" specifically? Let us read the verses that directly relate it:

> [Rev 10:2] And he had in his hand *a little book* open: and he set his right foot upon the *sea*, and his left foot on the *earth*,
> [Rev 10:8] And the voice which I heard from heaven spake unto me again, and said, Go and take the *little book* which is open in the hand of the angel which standeth upon the *sea* and upon the *earth*.
> [Rev 10:9] And I went unto the angel, and said unto him, Give me the *little book*. And he said unto me, Take it, and eat it up; and it shall make thy belly bitter, but it shall be in thy mouth sweet as honey.
> [Rev 10:10] And I took the *little book* out of the angel's hand, and ate it up; and it was in my mouth sweet as honey: and as soon as I had eaten it, my belly was bitter.

Verses 2 and 8 indicate that the mighty angel stands upon the sea and the earth, with his right foot upon the former and his left upon the latter. Such distinct positioning is emphasized when the "little book" is introduced in these verses, suggesting an important link between the positioning and the nature of the "little book."

To understand the meaning of such positioning, it is important to know what the "sea" and the "earth" signify. Let us first examine what the "sea" may refer to.

> [Rev 13:1] And I stood upon the sand of the *sea*, and saw a beast rise up out of the *sea*, having seven heads and ten horns, and upon his horns ten crowns, and upon his heads the name of blasphemy.

The verse above shows that the beast, or the Antichrist, comes out of the sea. In chapter 7 of this volume, the relation between the "sea" and the "bottomless pit" was suggested, as the beast came out of both as written in Revelation 11:7 and 13:1. In the context in Revelation 13:1, however, the "sea" is related to "(heathen) nations," as has been interpreted in the following commentaries. *Adam Clarke's Commentary on the Bible* writes: "the sea is therefore the symbol of a great multitude of nations, as has already been proved."[8] Also, Albert Barnes' *Notes on the Bible* writes:

> And I stood upon the sand of the sea—The sand upon the shore of the sea. That is, he seemed to stand there, and then had a vision of a beast rising out of the waters. The reason of this representation may, perhaps, have been that among the ancients the sea was regarded as the appropriate place for the origin of huge and terrible monsters (Prof. Stuart, in loco). This vision strongly resembles that in Dan 7:2 ff, where the prophet saw four beasts coming up in succession from the sea. See the notes on that place. In Daniel, the four winds of heaven are described as striving upon the great sea Dan 7:2, and the agitated ocean represents

the nations in commotion, or in a state of disorder and anarchy, and the four beasts represent four successive kingdoms that would spring up. See the notes on Dan 7:2. In the passage before us, John indeed describes no storm or tempest; but the sea itself, as compared with the land (see the notes on Rev 13:11), represents an agitated or unsettled state of things, and we should naturally look for that in the rise of the power here referred to. If the reference be to the civil or secular Roman power that has always appeared in connection with the papacy, and that has always followed its designs, then it is true that it rose amidst the agitations of the world, and from a state of commotion that might well be represented by the restless ocean. The sea in either case naturally describes a nation or people, for this image is frequently so employed in the Scriptures. Compare, as above, Dan 7:2, and Psa 65:7; Jer 51:42; Isa 60:5; Rev 10:2. The natural idea, therefore, in this passage, would be that the power that was represented by the "beast" would spring up among the nations, when restless or unsettled, like the waves of the ocean.[9]

The commentaries suggest that the "sea" in Revelation 10:2 refers to "nations." If "sea" signifies "nations," then the significance of the "earth" most likely could be identified as well. Another significance of the "sea" in Revelation 10:2 can be found in the meaning of its original Greek word, "θάλασσα (*thalassa*)." In addition to the meaning, "the sea in general," the Greek word has a specific meaning, "the Mediterranean Sea or the Red Sea."[10]

The mighty angel in Revelation chapter 10 has his right foot upon the sea and left foot on the earth. The Seven-Year Treaty, which is most possibly declared in Revelation chapter 10, is the covenant to be made between Israel and many nations as prophesied in Daniel chapter 9. If the "sea" in Revelation 10:2 signifies the Mediterranean Sea, then the "earth" next to it would most likely be referring to Israel, among all countries surrounding the Mediterranean Sea.

The specific definition of the "sea" being the Mediterranean Sea establishes the likely significance of the "earth" in Revelation chapter 10 as Israel. The "earth" being Israel, the connotation or the use of the word "sea" in Revelation chapter 10 as "nations" may be interpreted as nations excluding Israel, namely, the heathen nations.

Reinterpreting Revelation chapter 10 verses 2 and 8, the "little book" is open as the mighty angel stands on both the nations and Israel. In other words, the "little book" is related to the nation of Israel as well as the Gentiles. Such diametric construct of two parties implies the political situation that the Antichrist-to-be will take advantage of in confirming the covenant between Israel and many nations.

If verses 2 and 8 suggest such political stance related to the "little book," what do verses 9 and 10 reveal about the book?

> [Rev 10:9] And I went unto the angel, and said unto him, Give me the *little book*. And he said unto me, Take it, and *eat* it up; and it shall make thy belly bitter, but it shall be in thy mouth sweet as honey.
>
> [Rev 10:10] And I took the *little book* out of the angel's hand, and *ate* it up; and it was in my mouth sweet as honey: and as soon as I had eaten it, my belly was bitter.

As he is told to, John takes the book from the angel and eats it. Similar cases happened to Jeremiah, author of Psalms, and Ezekiel as in the following Scriptures:

[Jer 15:16] Thy words were found, and I did *eat* them; and thy word was unto me the *joy* and *rejoicing* of mine heart: for I am called by thy name, O LORD God of hosts.

Jeremiah confessed that God's words he ate were joy and delight of his heart.

[Ps 19:10] More to be desired are they than gold, yea, than much fine gold: *sweeter also than honey and the honeycomb.*

[Ps 119:103] How sweet are thy *words* unto my taste! yea, *sweeter than honey* to my mouth!

The confession of the author of these psalms is like that of Jeremiah in that His words are sweeter than honey. Ezekiel's case is comparable to John's: a scroll was given to him to eat as the little book was to John:

[Eze 2:9] And when I looked, behold, an hand was sent unto me; and, lo, a *roll of a book* was therein;

[Eze 2:10] And he spread it before me; and it was written within and without: and there was written therein lamentations, and mourning, and woe.

[Eze 3:1] Moreover he said unto me, Son of man, *eat* that thou findest; *eat this roll*, and go speak unto the house of Israel.

[Eze 3:2] So I opened my mouth, and he caused me to *eat that roll.*

[Eze 3:3] And he said unto me, Son of man, cause thy belly to *eat*, and fill thy bowels with this *roll* that I give thee. Then did I *eat* it; and it was in my mouth as *honey for sweetness.*

Judging by the sweet honey taste, what Ezekiel ate was undoubtedly the words of God. God's words are always sweet to His saints, as God is love. Yet, what God reveals through His words can be of bitter message. Especially to the prophet who is to proclaim God's judgment to the fallen mankind, words relating to the pouring of His wrath are bitter in the stomach to digest.

In Ezekiel, there is no description that the words of God turned bitter in the stomach. As for John, he realized God's message given to him was wrathful in nature, with disasters prepared for the last days, which turned bitter in the stomach in the end. After eating the little book, John must have realized that the prophecies in it entail the emergence of the Antichrist, the persecution of the saints of the Most High, the unrepentant multitude despite the calamities, and the pouring of God's wrath in the final days, which tormented John.

After John eats the little book, he is told that the prophecies must be delivered again:

[Rev 10:11] And he said unto me, Thou must *prophesy again* before many peoples, and nations, and tongues, and kings.

When are the contents of the little book prophesied again? The little book must have contained prophecies on events that would occur after Revelation chapter 10, most likely including those to occur during the final seven-year period. If Revelation chapter 10 surely were describing the confirmation of the Seven-Year Treaty, then chapter 11 would be describing the events following the confirmation of the Treaty. The things John wrote of in Revelation from chapter 11 and forward must be the contents of the "little book" that are prophesied again, relating to the last seven years and thereafter.

So far in this chapter, the following facts have been established: the fact that the final seven-year period is described from

Revelation chapter 11 and forward; the likelihood that the mighty angel who comes with the little book is Gabriel, who had delivered important messages including the prophecy on seventy weeks determined upon Israelites and Jerusalem in Daniel chapter 9; and the fact that the little book is pertinent to the relationship between Israel and Gentile nations. These support the interpretation that in Revelation chapter 10 God alerts readers of the beginning of the final seven-year period, reminding them of the prophecy from Daniel chapter 9, particularly that of the last seventieth week.

Most likely, God's intention is to have the presentation of the little book in Revelation chapter 10 serve as a wake-up call for mankind, particularly the believers, about the final seven-year period, the contents of which are detailed in Revelation chapters 11 and on. The events therein will be revealed in full as the day of the Lord approaches near.

The Seven Thunders

In Revelation chapter 10, John sees the little book and hears the seven thunders. The contents of the little book in Revelation chapter 10 are detailed or prophesied again in the chapters that follow. In contrast, God forbids John from writing down what "the seven thunders" utter and tells him to seal them up. Such difference indicates that the contents of the seven thunders and the little book are not the same. What are the seven thunders?

> [Rev 10:3] And cried with a loud voice, as when a lion roareth: and when he had cried, [*the*] *seven thunders* uttered their voices.
>
> [Rev 10:4] And when *the seven thunders* had uttered their voices, I was about to write: and I heard a voice from heaven saying unto me, Seal up those things which *the seven thunders* uttered, and write them not.

Like the "little book," "the seven thunders" are affiliated with the mighty angel who stands upon both the "sea" and the "earth." Therefore, like the "little book," "the seven thunders" are most likely related to the nations of Israel and the Gentiles.

The Scripture clearly indicates that the seven thunders are not just some phenomena in themselves, but are what can utter voices. John hears the voices, but the contents of the uttered voices are forbidden from being written down.

What could the contents be about? Since God had the voices of the thunders in Revelation chapter 10 be sealed up, their detailed contents will be revealed only at the time they are actually executed. In other words, time will tell what the contents are, when the corresponding incident finally occurs in the future.

The nature of the contents, however, can be understood before they transpire, when the meanings of the words "seven" and "thunder" are examined.

First, the following passages shed light on the characteristics of "the thunders":

> [Job 26:14] Lo, these are parts of his ways: but how little a portion is heard of him? but the *thunder* (רַעַם, *ra`am*) of his power who can understand?
>
> [Ps 77:18] The voice of thy *thunder* (רַעַם, *ra`am*) was in the heaven: the lightnings lightened the world: the earth trembled and shook.
>
> [Ps 81:7] Thou calledst in trouble, and I delivered thee; I answered thee in the secret place of *thunder* (רַעַם, *ra`am*): I proved thee at the waters of Meribah. Selah.
>
> [Ps 104:7] At thy rebuke they fled; at the voice of thy *thunder* (רַעַם, *ra`am*) they hasted away.
>
> [Isa 29:6] Thou shalt be visited of the LORD of hosts with *thunder* (רַעַם, *ra`am*), and with earthquake, and great noise, with storm and tempest, and the flame of devouring fire.

The Scriptures above indicate that, in general, thunder is associated with God's power. The commentaries agree and state that thunder is "strong and powerful voice of God,"[11] and "that in the ragings of the storm, or of the whirlwind, the voice of God was heard—the deep bellowing thunder—as if God spoke to people."[12]

Second, the number "seven" is identified with divine perfection and completion. Such numerological symbolism is derived from the creation week in Genesis when God spent six days to create the heavens and the earth and rested on the seventh day.

Incorporating such characteristics to the interpretation suggests that the seven thunders will manifest God's power, His Almighty Sovereignty, in completely fulfilling His promises and plan for His people and Jerusalem, as well as for the mankind.

What are His plans for the Israelites and the mankind? Are the "seven thunders" identified with a new prophecy or promise determined by God? Examining the Scripture in the original Greek language suggests that this is not the case.

> [Rev 10:3] And cried with a loud voice, as when a lion roareth: and when he had cried, [the] seven thunders (αἱ ἑπτὰ βρονταὶ, hai hepta brontai) uttered their voices.

As can be seen above, the "seven thunders" in the original Greek contain the definite article "the (αἱ, hai)" in the front. This suggests that "[the] seven thunders" are something that the readers are already aware of. In other words, the thing related to "the seven thunders" is not introduced in Revelation for the first time, but rather, had been told before in the Scripture. Then, what could that be? When did God tell something related to "the seven thunders" before?

To answer this question, it is important to remember that what God has determined to accomplish in the last days are all summed up in the final week, the last seven-year period. God had appointed this time in order to bring the mankind, especially the Israelites, to know Him. Through the determined wars, desolations, and plagues, God truly wants people to humble themselves and repent unto life. Again, the prophecy on this final week was provided in the book of Daniel:

> [Da 9:24] *Seventy weeks are determined* upon thy people and upon thy holy city, to finish the transgression, and to make an end of sins, and to make reconciliation for iniquity, and to bring in everlasting righteousness, and to seal up the vision and prophecy, and to anoint the most Holy.

Among the seventy weeks determined in Daniel, the final seventieth week remains to be fulfilled. What God had determined for His people, Israelites, and His city, Jerusalem, shall come to pass during the last period of mankind's six millennia of history, just before the return of Jesus Christ. This is where the significance of the "seven thunders" can be found in relation to the fulfillment of the final seven-year period.

The onset of the prophecy regarding the last week of mankind in Daniel is marked by "[the] seven thunders" in Revelation chapter 10 as the time for its fulfillment is at hand. In fact, right after the seven thunders utter their voices, the mighty angel warns that "there should be time no longer" (Rev 10:6) until the fulfillment of the prophecies on the final seven-year period. In other words, the seven thunders uttering their voices will mark the beginning of the fulfillment of the prophecies in the "little book," which are prophesied again in Revelation chapter 11 and forward.

If the "seven thunders" mark the beginning of the final seven-year period, what is the equivalent marker that is foretold in the prophecy in Daniel?

[Da 9:27] And he shall confirm the covenant with many for *one week*: and in the midst of the week he shall cause the sacrifice and the oblation to cease, and for the overspreading of abominations he shall make it desolate, even until the consummation, and that determined shall be poured upon the desolate.

The verse above shows that the final "one week" starts with the Antichrist-to-be's confirming the covenant with many. As discussed before, the "seven thunders" concern the relationship between Israel and the nations of the Gentiles, and the completion of God's plan for Israelites, Jerusalem, and the mankind. When the Antichrist's covenant is confirmed, the final seven-year period will commence. After the seven thunders utter their voices, the contents of the little book will be executed.

The "seven thunders" will mark the arrival of God's appointed time for fulfilling the seventieth week. Their "voices" they utter, then, will probably be the contents of the Seven-Year Treaty, sealed up until they are revealed at the time the Antichrist-to-be confirms the covenant. The "seven thunders" in Revelation chapter 10 are immediately followed by the fulfillment of the prophecies in the "little book," or the commencement of the final seven-year period.

[Rev 10:6] And sware by him that liveth for ever and ever, who created heaven, and the things that therein are, and the earth, and the things that therein are, and the sea, and the things which are therein, that *there should be time no longer:*

Why does the mighty angel (Gabriel) announce "there should be time no longer" in Revelation chapter 10? It is because the confirmation of the covenant in the final week would start the countdown of the seven-year period until the Lord will return toward its end. As the final seven years expire, God's planned history for salvation of the mankind will also come to completion.

The Mystery of God

In Revelation 10:6, the mighty angel calls attention to the immediate imminence of the seven-year period. Yet, in verse 7, before he tells John to eat the little book to prophesy its contents again, he specially mentions that when the seventh trumpet is sounded, the mystery of God will be finished.

> [Rev 10:7] But in the days of the voice of the seventh angel, when he shall begin to sound, the *mystery* (μυστήριον, *mystērion*) of God should be finished, *as he hath declared* (εὐαγγελίζω, *euaggelizō*) to his servants the prophets.

As the passage indicates, this "mystery" event should be something His servants and prophets anticipate to occur and be finished in the last days, as God had declared. This must be a very important event that the believers should pay attention to, and it is precisely for this reason that the mighty angel does not forget to specifically point this event out among all events of the seven-year period that is about to commence.

What does this mystery of God entail? The passage is stating that although the mystery of God was declared to His servants the prophets before, it will finally come to finish at the time of the seventh angel's sounding. The original Greek word of "declared" in the verse is εὐαγγελίζω (*euaggelizō*), which is usually translated in the King James Version Bible as to "preach the gospel" and means "to bring good news."[13] As the Scripture indicates, the "mystery of God" is good news that had been declared to believers but has not been accomplished yet. What then could this "mystery of God" be?

[Ro 11:25] For I would not, brethren, that ye should be ignorant of this *mystery*, lest ye should be wise in your own conceits; that *blindness in part is happened to Israel, until the fulness of the Gentiles be come in.*

The verse above writes of one kind of mystery, that Israel will be saved only after the number of Gentile believers will first reach fullness. This coincides with what Jesus Christ told about the end of this world:

[Mt 24:14] And this *gospel of the kingdom* shall be preached in all the world for a witness *unto all nations*; and then shall the end come.

The Lord specified that the end shall come when the gospel is preached to all the nations. But there is another kind of mystery that needs to be understood in order to interpret Revelation 10:7.

[1Co 15:51] Behold, I shew you a *mystery*; We shall not all sleep, but we shall all be *changed*,
[1Co 15:52] In a moment, in the twinkling of an eye, *at the last trump*: for the trumpet shall sound, and the dead shall be raised incorruptible, and we shall be *changed*.

According to the passage above, the mystery in question deals with the changing of the corruptible bodies into the incorruptible at the time of the rapture. This change into the incorruptible bodies is critical for His saints, for that will occur when they will be raptured to meet with Christ:

[Eph 5:31] For this cause shall a man leave his father and mother, and shall be joined unto his wife, and they two shall be one flesh.

[Eph 5:32] This is a *great mystery*: but I speak
concerning *Christ and the church*.

What is addressed by the term "great mystery" in the passage
above is the relationship between Christ and the church, His body.
The rapture is indeed a part of the "great mystery" not only
because this is when the corruptible bodies will be changed into
the incorruptible, but also because this is when His bride, the
church, will meet her groom, Christ, in the air.

For this reason, the "mystery of God" is announced in
Revelation 10:7, 3.5 years before the seventh trumpet will actually
be sounded in Revelation 11:15. With the seventh trumpet
mentioned in Revelation 10:7 being the one and only exception,
never in other Revelation's events of the seals, the trumpets, and
the bowls, is the next event in sequence announced, foretold, or
forewarned in advance (the warning of the three woes in
Revelation 8:13, 9:12, and 11:14 are not taken into consideration).
This is to say, God really wants the readers to fathom and pay
attention to this "mystery," so that one can even prepare for it in
expectation. To neglect or to fail to recognize this "mystery of God"
will result in a great loss to a believer.

[Col 1:27] To whom God would make known what is
the riches of the glory of this *mystery* among the
Gentiles; which is *Christ* in you, the hope of glory:

The passage here introduces another "mystery," which is
defined as the indwelling of Christ in Gentiles. If the indwelling of
Jesus Christ among the Gentiles while living on earth is a
"mystery," how much of greater hope and mystery would rapture
or meeting with Christ in the air be?

Finally, there is another kind of mystery in the Bible, a mystery
of antithetic nature to those already discussed:

[2Th 2:7] For the *mystery of iniquity* doth already work: only he who now *letteth will let, until he be taken* out of the way.

[2Th 2:8] And then shall that *Wicked [the Antichrist] be revealed*, whom the Lord shall consume with the spirit of his mouth, and shall destroy with the brightness of his coming:

In contrast to the "mystery of God," the above passage heralds the "mystery of iniquity." Nonetheless, this mystery is also related to the rapture. "He who now letteth will let" (the one who now holds it back will continue to do so—NIV) in verse 7 most probably refers to those who "overcome" in Revelation, especially those who get raptured (caught up unto God) in chapter 12, who are collectively represented by "a man child," who is "to rule all nations with a rod of iron." The detailed interpretations and proofs behind these statements on the rapture will be disclosed in the next volume. In any case, the abovementioned passage indicates that there are overcomers who are holding back the "mystery of iniquity," the works of the wicked Antichrist, until they are "taken out of the way" via the rapture.

As scrutinized above, the passages about the "mystery" in the New Testament can be interpreted in relations to the rapture. In accord with this view is the interpretation of Revelation 10:7 that the finishing of the mystery of God refers to the timing of the rapture during the sounding of the seventh trumpet:

[Rev 10:7] But in the days of the voice of the *seventh* angel, when he shall begin to *sound*, the *mystery* of God should be finished, as he hath declared to his servants the prophets.

The following passages also show that the seventh trumpet is undeniably connected to the rapture.

[1Th 4:16] For the Lord himself shall descend from heaven with a shout, with the voice of the archangel, and with the *trump* of God: and the *dead in Christ shall rise* first:
[1Th 4:17] Then we which are alive and remain shall be *caught up* together with them in the clouds, to *meet the Lord in the air*: and so shall we ever be with the Lord.

The "trump" in verse 16 refers to the seventh trumpet, and the rising of the dead in Christ refers to the changing of the corruptible to the incorruptible bodies. Verse 17 above speaks of the rapture, when the alive in Christ also are transformed into the incorruptible bodies and are caught up.

[Rev 11:15] And the *seventh* angel *sounded*; and there were great voices in heaven, saying, *The kingdoms of this world are become the kingdoms of our Lord, and of his Christ*; and he shall reign for ever and ever.

As can be seen in the passage above, the time for the "kingdoms of this world are [to] become the kingdoms of our Lord, and of his Christ" comes soon after the rapture that occurs when the seventh trumpet is sounded. The establishment of the kingdoms of our Lord and Christ is ultimately consummated when Christ Jesus returns to the earth. After Christ's return, He will establish the "millennial kingdom" on this earth to rule for thousand years, and then finally "a new heaven and a new earth" will come.

[Rev 20:4] And I saw thrones, and they sat upon them, and judgment was given unto them: and I saw the souls of them that were beheaded for the witness of Jesus, and for the word of God, and which had not worshipped the beast, neither his image, neither had received his mark upon their foreheads, or in their hands; and they lived and reigned with Christ *a thousand years*.

[Rev 21:1] And I saw *a new heaven and a new earth*: for the first heaven and the first earth were passed away; and there was no more sea.

Obviously, both the "millennial kingdom" and "a new heaven and a new earth" will not be of this world but will be of the Lord's, because they will be the result of Jesus' second coming.

It is important to understand that the "kingdoms of our Lord, and of his Christ" in Revelation 11:15 are finally established when the Lord establishes the "millennial kingdom" upon His return to the earth. This ends the "kingdoms of this world" (Rev 11:15) forever, and the millennial kingdom of our Lord and Christ comes. When "a new heaven and a new earth" come after the "millennial kingdom," the "kingdoms of this world" will have already been non-existent for a thousand years. Therefore, Revelation 11:15 speaks of the time at which the millennial kingdom starts, not ends—"the kingdoms of this world are [to] become the kingdoms of our Lord" (Rev 11:15).

The imminence of Lord's return to the earth is proclaimed in Revelation 11:15 at the sounding of the seventh trumpet, as the Lord returns at the end of the seven-year period, the latter half of which will contain the seven bowls of God's wrath that will destroy the destroyers of the earth.

[Rev 11:18] And the nations were angry, and thy wrath is come, and the time of the dead, that they should be judged, and that thou shouldest give reward unto thy servants the prophets, and to the saints, and them that fear thy name, small and great; and shouldest *destroy them which destroy the earth*.

If Jesus comes after all the seven bowls have been poured, why is His return already mentioned at the seventh trumpet? This can be understood upon reading the following Scripture about the seventh seal:

[Rev 8:1] And when he had opened the *seventh seal*, there was silence in heaven about the space of half an hour.
[Rev 8:2] And I saw the seven angels which stood before God; and to them were given *seven trumpets*.
[Rev 8:6] And the seven angels which had the *seven trumpets* prepared themselves to sound.

The passage above shows that when the seventh seal was opened, seven trumpets were prepared to be sounded. This may indicate that the sounding of the seven trumpets occurs during the period of the seventh seal, the last one in the seal series. However, the seventh seal and the seven trumpet events are distinct from each other and occur at different times, without overlap of time. In other words, before the seven trumpet events occur, the seventh seal event is fulfilled as the phenomena of voices, thunderings, lightnings, and an earthquake (Rev 8:5).

Similarly, the pouring of the seven bowls occurs during the period of the seventh trumpet, the last one in the trumpet series. The seventh trumpet is accompanied by the phenomena including lightnings, voices, thunderings, an earthquake, and great hail (Rev 11:19) that occur before the seven bowls are poured. The seven bowls occur in the latter half of the final seven-year period during the period of the seventh trumpet, and the return of Jesus to the earth also occurs toward the end of the latter 3.5 years. This could explain why the return of Jesus to establish His kingdom that comes after the pouring of seven bowls is mentioned at the sounding of the seventh trumpet.

In any case, the "mystery" of rapture is declared about 3.5 years in advance at the beginning of the seven-year period (Rev 10:7), and the Lord's return to the earth is also proclaimed about 3.5 years in advance (Rev 11:15). Both events are emphasized for their utmost significance and imminence. Indeed, starting from the Seven-Year Treaty until the return of Jesus Christ, with the sounding of the seventh trumpet in the middle, there should be time no longer (Rev 10:6), as the Antichrist and nations will gather to act out evil, leading to God's pouring of wrath and eventual return of the Lord on the earth.

Revelation Chapter 10 is about the Seven-Year Treaty

So far, the chapter explored whether the pivotal prophecy on the final week was found among the apocalyptic writings of Revelation. It is more than correct to assume that the book of Revelation would contain the writings about the final week determined for Israelites and Jerusalem as written in Daniel, especially when considering the book of Revelation is mostly dedicated to the end-time prophecies.

The fact that the descriptive time expressions with regard to the timeline of the final seven years appear starting from chapter 11 confirmed that Revelation chapter 10 could be describing the Seven-Year Treaty, which marks the beginning of the final seven-year period.

The sixth trumpet is the second woe (Rev 9:12; 11:14), which starts with WWIII and ends with the prophesying of the two witnesses for 3.5 years. The descriptions of WWIII are written in Revelation chapter 9, whereas those of the two witnesses are written in chapter 11. Between the two chapters appears chapter 10, which writes of the Seven-Year Treaty that marks the beginning of the final seventieth week.

This signifies that the Seven-Year Treaty will be confirmed after WWIII and will most likely mark the end of WWIII. The treaty will involve Israel and many nations, and it will probably mark the beginning of a different political era with a new hegemonic system in place (so called New World Order), similar to the time when the United Nations emerged out of WWII.

As previously mentioned, the prophesying of the two witnesses in Revelation 11 is a part of the sixth trumpet. As it is partly related to the rapture, this event will be discussed in the next volume.

This interpretation of Revelation chapter 10 as containing the Seven-Year Treaty had already been proclaimed on the authors' YouTube channel in 2015. In this regard, the authors may be one of the first to interpret Revelation chapter 10 as containing the Seven-Year Treaty.

CHAPTER 10.
THE SEVENTH TRUMPET:
A GREAT HAIL

The latter portion of Revelation chapter 11 is about the seventh trumpet, which comes quickly after the "second woe" has passed (Rev 11:14).

> [Rev 11:15] And the seventh angel sounded; and there were great voices in heaven, saying, The kingdoms of this world are become the kingdoms of our Lord, and of His Christ; and He shall reign for ever and ever.
> [Rev 11:16] And the four and twenty elders, which sat before God on their seats, fell upon their faces, and worshipped God,
> [Rev 11:17] Saying, We give Thee thanks, O Lord God Almighty, which art, and wast, and art to come; because Thou hast taken to Thee Thy great power, and hast reigned.
> [Rev 11:18] And the nations were angry, and Thy wrath is come, and the time of the dead, that they should be judged, and that Thou shouldest give *reward unto Thy servants* the prophets, and to the saints, and them that fear Thy name, small and great; and shouldest destroy them which destroy the earth.
> [Rev 11:19] And the *temple of God was opened* in heaven, and there was seen in His temple the ark of His

testament: and there were *lightnings, and voices, and thunderings, and an earthquake, and great hail.*

The Seventh Trumpet: Lightnings, Voices, Thunderings, an Earthquake, and Great Hail

The seventh trumpet is the last trumpet, when the rapture will happen. Therefore, in verse 19 the temple of God is opened in heaven. The opening of the temple in heaven signifies that someone is ready to enter the place. The descriptions in verse 18—"to reward God's servants, the prophets, the saints and those who fear God's name"—further substantiate that this is the time for rapture.

The detailed study on the rapture that occurs at the seventh trumpet will be provided in the next volume. In this volume, only the natural phenomena that will occur at the seventh trumpet will be expounded.

While the four phenomena (lightnings, voices, thunderings, earthquake) occur during the seventh seal, the seventh trumpet, and the seventh bowl events, they are not identical events.

For example, in the seventh seal, there is no hail at all. In the seventh trumpet, however, "great hail" is an addition not present in the seventh seal. Also, the earthquake in the seventh bowl is said to be the greatest in magnitude that mankind has ever seen, rendering it a clearly distinct earthquake from those in the seventh seal and the seventh trumpet. This is made clear in the following verse:

[Rev 16:18] And there were voices, and thunders, and lightnings; and there was a great earthquake, *such as was not since men were upon the earth,* so mighty an earthquake, and so great.

Furthermore, there are different degrees of "great hail" in the seventh trumpet and the seventh bowl. In fact, the weight of the hailstone in the seventh bowl is that of a talent, as described as follows:

> [Rev 16:21] And there fell upon men a *great hail* out of heaven, every stone about the weight of a *talent*: and men blasphemed God because of the plague of the hail; for the plague thereof was exceeding great.

This description makes it clear that the great hail in the seventh bowl is an exceedingly "great hail," different from that of the seventh trumpet. Bear in mind that there was no object falling on the earth from the sky in the event of the seventh seal. The "great hail" during the seventh trumpet shown in Revelation 11:19 will actually involve some substantially weighty objects falling from the sky. A possibility of an impact from the outer space, then, cannot be overruled. Furthermore, these falling objects in the seventh trumpet will certainly be less than a hundred pounds, the weight of each hailstone of the seventh bowl.

In the Tunguska explosion, the seventh seal, the blast was speculated to have been caused by a meteorite of certain size that only reached the Earth's atmosphere and exploded in the air. Nonetheless, the effect was so great that the incident is known as the first "impact" in history. Then, if something actually hits Earth in the seventh trumpet, as the "great hail" indicates, what might be the effects of the true impact?

It is interesting that after the Tunguska blast, no scientist or explorer could find any signs of a crater having been formed. A crater would have formed if the fragment of a meteorite actually hit Earth. Scientists came to the conclusion that the matter had actually exploded in the atmosphere based upon the fact that there was no crater found at the site of the Tunguska blast. Yet, the effects of the blast were "voices," "thunderings," "lightnings," and "an earthquake," as described in Revelation 8:5 and discussed in Volume 1.

Could this mean that when the seventh trumpet is sounded, something similar of origin but bigger in size than the one in the seventh seal would directly strike Earth and cause all of these effects of the seventh seal in greater magnitude? When a fragment of a meteoroid or a comet hits Earth, an earthquake would be a natural consequence.

What about lightnings, voices, and thunderings? Based on the descriptions in Revelation and the interpretations so far, the natural phenomena of the seventh trumpet may presumably be similar to what were accounted for the seventh seal. A similar prediction can be found as follows:

In a detailed scientific article entitled "The Great Siberian Meteorite: An Account of the most Remarkable Astronomical Event of the Twentieth Century," in *Scientific American* (July 1928), Chas P. Olivier of the International Astronomical Association wrote: "Fortunately for humanity, this meteoric fall [Tunguska blast] happened in a region where there were no inhabitants . . . but if such a thing can happen in Siberia there is no known reason why the same could not happen in the United States."[1]

In fact, in the seventh seal, even when there was no contact or collision of the meteorite with Earth, the momentum that the meteorite brought into the atmosphere of Earth as it exploded still caused the effects—voices, thunderings, lightnings, and an earthquake. These phenomena will most likely occur in the seventh trumpet and the seventh bowl as well, in a similar fashion but with greater magnitudes.

As discussed in Volume 1, the "voices" were strange gunfire-like sounds distinct from the thundering sounds, and the "lightnings" were the bright glows in the night sky, and the "earthquake" was the presence of seismic waves around Earth.

What is interesting is that in the seventh trumpet and the seventh bowl, the phenomena of voices, thunderings, lightnings, and an earthquake, occur before the hail hits the earth. In the seventh trumpet, these phenomena are described first before the great hail in the Scripture:

> [Rev 11:19] And the temple of God was opened in heaven, and there was seen in His temple the ark of His testament: and there were *lightnings*, and *voices*, and *thunderings*, and an *earthquake*, and great hail.

Likewise, in the seventh bowl, these phenomena are described before the "plague of the hail" in Revelation chapter 16.

What is the significance of the order of description? It refers to the order of occurrence of these phenomena. In the seventh seal, these phenomena occurred without an actual impact occurring:

> [Rev 8:5] And the angel took the censer, and filled it with fire of the altar, and cast it into the earth: and there were *voices*, and *thunderings*, and *lightnings*, and an *earthquake*.

As discussed in Volume 1, these phenomena occurred as something like a meteorite exploded in the atmosphere, creating pressure, heat, and sounds associated with it. This incident shows that with the momentum the meteorite brings into the atmosphere of Earth, these effects are natural consequences. Therefore, before the hail hits the earth in the seventh trumpet and the seventh bowl, these phenomena of voices, thunderings, lightnings, and an earthquake, will first occur—that is, as something like a meteoroid enters the Earth's atmosphere.

The hail could be a meteorite and its fragments hitting the earth after its explosion in the air as in the seventh seal. With the case of an actual contact with material from the outer space, a crater would form at the site of impact. Would the sounding of the seventh trumpet result in a record-breaking, astronomical meteorite impact? Only time will tell.

Today, there are many worried scientists and observers reporting fast-approaching asteroids or comets that could potentially hit Earth and cause a massive destruction and death toll. At the same time, there are active discussions on ways to deter or avert them from hitting Earth.

Planetary objects that caused much fuss internationally include the Planet X or Nibiru.[2] Although this did not come to hit planet Earth, many people around the world feared that such planetary collision may be associated with the fulfillment of some end-time prophecies.

A news report had mentioned a doomsday set on February of 2012 due to a collision of Earth with an approaching asteroid named 2012 DA14. According to the report, NASA confirmed that the asteroid was 60 meters or 197 feet in size and would reach the shortest distance from planet Earth on February 15, 2013.[3]

The problem that this kind of asteroid poses is the potential destruction that it will incur in case it crashes into Earth. It is expected to result in a considerable impact similar to that of the Tunguska blast.[4] If such collisions between Earth and a planetary object ever occur in the future with significant magnitude, the first one would be the seventh trumpet, and the latter one, particularly the one with the greatest magnitude, would be the seventh bowl.

The Seventh Bowl: Voices, Thunders, Lightnings, a Great Earthquake, and a Great Hail

As mentioned earlier, similar natural phenomena occur in the seventh seal, the seventh trumpet, and the seventh bowl. The Scripture regarding the seventh bowl is as follows:

[Rev 16:17] And the seventh angel poured out his vial into the air; and there came a great voice out of the temple of heaven, from the throne, saying, It is done.

[Rev 16:18] And there were *voices*, and *thunders*, and *lightnings*; and there was a *great earthquake*, such as was not since men were upon the earth, so mighty an earthquake, and so great.

[Rev 16:19] And the great city was divided into three parts, and the cities of the nations fell: and great Babylon came in remembrance before God, to give unto her the cup of the wine of the fierceness of his wrath.

[Rev 16:20] And every island fled away, and the mountains were not found.

[Rev 16:21] And there fell upon men a *great hail* out of heaven, every stone about the weight of a *talent*: and men blasphemed God because of the *plague of the hail*; for the plague thereof was exceeding great.

The effects of both the seventh seal and the seventh trumpet have been identified previously. But they are not comparable with those of the seventh bowl. The effects of the seventh bowl are described as tremendously catastrophic, to the extent that they significantly surpass those of the seventh seal and the seventh trumpet. As Revelation 16:18 warns, not only "voices, and thunders, and lightnings" but also "a great earthquake" on an unprecedented scale in history will occur. As the meteorite explodes in the air, "voices, thunders, and lightnings" will occur. The earthquake here will probably be caused by the explosion and impact of the meteorite with Earth. The magnitude of this earthquake will be far greater than that of any earthquake in history.

As a result of such a great earthquake, the great city (possibly the city of "MYSTERY, BABYLON THE GREAT" in Revelation 17:5, most likely Rome[5]) will be divided into three parts, the cities of the nations will fall, as described in Revelation 16:19. In verse 20, every island and mountain will be swept away. Then, in verse 21, "a great hail" will fall "out of heaven, every stone about the weight of a talent." A "talent" in this context refers to "a talent of silver weighed about 100 pounds or 45 kg" or "a talent of gold, 200 pounds or 91 kg."[6]

If the great city destroyed by the great earthquake is the city of "MYSTERY, BABYLON THE GREAT," then the destruction of the city is also found in Revelation 18.

> [Rev 18:21] And a mighty angel took up *a stone like a great millstone*, and cast it into the sea, saying, Thus with violence shall that great city Babylon be thrown down, and shall be found no more at all.

If the "stone like a great millstone" that the mighty angel casts is the cause of the great hail in the seventh bowl, then the great hail would be the meteorite and its fragments from the explosion in the air. If the hail falls into the sea only, there will be no direct plague upon the earth, and the expression "the plague thereof was exceeding great" would not be possible. The main body of the meteorite, "a stone like a great millstone," will be cast into the sea, while the debris after the explosion will fall onto the earth.

The Scripture describes the yet unrepentant survivors—"men blasphemed God because of the plague of the hail" (Rev 16:21). If the interpretation on the seventh seal was correct in the previous volume, further extrapolation would render that a huge, massive, gigantic meteorite will hit Earth when the seventh bowl is poured.

This volume ends with the discourse on the seven trumpets by identifying the events as they occurred in history and exploring the possible future manifestations of events yet to occur. The topics on the rapture, the Antichrist, the wars in the final days, and the persecution of the saints on the earth start to appear in Revelation chapter 11. The details of these topics will be dealt with in the future volumes.

ENDNOTES

CHAPTER 1

[1] Kenneth Scott Latourette, *Christianity through the Ages* (New York: Harper & Row, 1965), Chapter 10.

[2] *Ibid.*

[3] Wilson, "Footnotes: Hezbollah, Hamas and Hatred of Jews," *Mercury Radio Arts*, June 1, 2011, accessed January 13, 2012, http://www.glennbeck.com/2011/06/01/footnotes-hezbollah-hamas-and-hatred-of-jews.

[4] Johann Jakob Herzog, Philip Schaff, and Albert Hauck, *The New Schaff-Herzog Encyclopedia of Religious Knowledge, Vol. VI: Innocents–Liudger* (New York, NY and London, England: Funk & Wagnalls, 1910), 177.

[5] *Ibid.*

[6] Simon Dubnov, *History of the Jews from the Roman Empire to the Early Medieval Period, Volume 2* (Thomas Yoseloff, Inc., 1968), 523–524.

[7] Herzog et al., *Encyclopedia of Religious Knowledge*, 177–178.

[8] *Ibid.*

[9] *Ibid.*

[10] *Ibid.*, 178.

[11] *Ibid.*

[12] *Ibid.*

[13] *Ibid.*

[14] Joseph L. Baron, *A Treasury of Jewish Quotations* (Rowman & Littlefield, 1996), 66.

[15] Isidore Singer, ed., "Conversion to Christianity," in *The Jewish Encyclopedia* (New York, NY and London, England: Funk & Wagnalls, 1906).

[16] Herzog et al., *Encyclopedia of Religious Knowledge,* 178.

[17] Singer, "Conversion to Christianity."

[18] Herzog et al., *Encyclopedia of Religious Knowledge,* 178.

[19] Singer, "Conversion to Christianity."

[20] *Ibid.*

[21] Herzog et al., *Encyclopedia of Religious Knowledge,* 178.

[22] W. T. Gidney, *The History of the London Society for Promoting Christianity Amongst the Jews: From 1809 to 1908* (London: London Society for Promoting Christianity Amongst the Jews, 1908), 27–29.

[23] *Ibid.*

[24] Herzog et al., *Encyclopedia of Religious Knowledge,* 178.

[25] "An Excerpt from Gerry Black, 'The Right School in the Right Place: The History of the Stepney Jewish School, 1864–2013,'" *Jewish Historical Studies* 45 (2013): 131–144, http://www.jstor.org/stable/23720246.

[26] *Ibid.*

[27] *Ibid.*

[28] Herzog et al., *Encyclopedia of Religious Knowledge,* 179.

[29] *Ibid.*

[30] *Ibid.,* 179–180.

[31] "Report of the First Lutheran Conference on Mission among Israel," *Chicago Local Committee on Mission among Israel* (1901): 78–85.

[32] Herzog et al., *Encyclopedia of Religious Knowledge,* 179–180.

[33] "Report of the First Lutheran Conference on Mission among Israel," 78–85.

[34] Herzog et al., *Encyclopedia of Religious Knowledge*, 179-180.

[35] "Report of the First Lutheran Conference on Mission among Israel," 78–85.

[36] Herzog et al., *Encyclopedia of Religious Knowledge*, 179–180.

[37] "Report of the First Lutheran Conference on Mission among Israel," 78–85.

[38] *Ibid.*

[39] Albert Montefiore Hyamson, *British projects for the restoration of the Jews* (Petty & Sons Ltd., 1917).

[40] Elizabeth E. Imber, "Saving Jews: The History of Jewish-Christian Relations in Scotland, 1880–1948," *A Master's Thesis*, Department of Near Eastern and Judaic Studies, Brandeis University, accessed May 13, 2015, http://bir.brandeis.edu/bitstream/handle/10192/23881/Saving+Jews.pdf?sequence=1.

[41] Herzog et al., *Encyclopedia of Religious Knowledge*, 180.

[42] Charles Henry Robinson, *History of Christian Missions* (New York: Charles Scribner's Sons, 1915), 475.

[43] Herzog et al., *Encyclopedia of Religious Knowledge*, 180.

[44] Ellen Ross, "'Playing Deaf': Jewish Women at the Medical Missions of East London, 1880–1920s," *19: Interdisciplinary Studies in the Long Nineteenth Century*, Birkbeck, University of London, accessed May 13, 2015, http://www.19.bbk.ac.uk/article/view/622/744.

[45] *Ibid.*

[46] Isidore Singer, ed., "Statistics," in *The Jewish Encyclopedia* (New York, NY and London, England: Funk & Wagnalls, 1906).

[47] Isidore Singer, ed., "Conversion to Christianity, Modern," in *The Jewish Encyclopedia* (New York, NY and London, England: Funk & Wagnalls, 1906).

[48] John Talbot Gracey, *The Missionary Year-book for 1889–90, Containing Historical and Statistical Accounts of the Principal*

Protestant Missionary Societies in America, Great Britain, and the Continent of Europe (New York: F.H. Revell, 1889), 244.

[49] Ross, "'Playing Deaf': Jewish Women."

[50] *Ibid.*

[51] Robinson, *History of Christian Missions*, 473.

[52] "Report of the First Lutheran Conference on Mission among Israel," 22–23.

[53] Singer, "Conversion to Christianity."

[54] "19th Century Anti-Semitism," *Alpha History*, July 19, 2012, accessed May 14, 2015, http://alphahistory.com/holocaust/19th-century-anti-semitism.

[55] *Ibid.*

[56] *Ibid.*

[57] *Ibid.*

[58] Herzog et al., *Encyclopedia of Religious Knowledge*, 181.

[59] Singer, "Conversion to Christianity."

[60] *Ibid.*

CHAPTER 2

[1] Marvin R. Vincent, *Vincent's Word Studies in the New Testament* (Peabody, MA: Hendrickson, 1888).

[2] Robert Jamieson, A. R. Fausset, and David Brown, *A Commentary on the Old and New Testaments* (1871).

[3] A. T. Robertson, *Word Pictures in the New Testament* (Nashville, Tenn.: Broadman, 1930).

[4] Adam Clarke, *Adam Clarke's Commentary on the Bible* (New York: Abingdon, 1829).

[5] John Gill, *John Gill's Exposition of the Entire Bible* (1746–1766).

[6] "Charles H. Spurgeon," *Bath Road Baptist Church*, accessed September 10, 2011, http://www.iclnet.org/pub/resources/text/history/spurgeon/sp-bio.html.

7 William P. Farley, "Charles Haddon Spurgeon: The Greatest Victorian Preacher," *Enrichment Journal*, The General Council of the Assemblies of God, accessed May 16, 2015, http://enrichmentjournal.ag.org/200701/200701_136_Spurgeon.cfm.

8 Alvyn Austin, *China's Millions* (Grand Rapids, Mich.: William B. Eerdmans Pub., 2007), 87–88.

9 Martyn McGeown, "The Life & Theology of D. L. Moody," *Covenant Protestant Reformed Church*, accessed September 10, 2011, http://www.cprf.co.uk/articles/moody.htm.

10 Diane Severance and Dan Graves, "Dwight L. Moody Was Converted," *Christianity.com*, accessed May 16, 2015, http://www.christianity.com/church/church-history/timeline/1801-1900/dwight-l-moody-was-converted-11630499.html.

11 McGeown, "The Life & Theology of D. L. Moody."

12 William R. Moody, *The Life of Dwight L. Moody*, The Official Authorized ed. (New York: Fleming H. Revell, 1900), 133–135.

13 Gerald H. Anderson, ed., *Biographical Dictionary of Christian Missions* (New York: Macmillan Reference USA, 1998), 230, 470–471.

14 Bruce J. Evensen, *God's Man for the Gilded Age D. L. Moody and the Rise of Modern Mass Evangelism* (Oxford: Oxford UP, 2003), 3.

15 George Müller, *A Narrative of Some of the Lord's Dealings with George Müller* (London: J. Nisbet, 1860).

16 *Ibid.*

17 *Ibid.*

18 *Ibid.*

19 "Scriptural Knowledge Institution," *Müllers*, The George Müller Charitable Trust, accessed May 16, 2015, http://www.mullers.org/find-out-more-1834.

[20] Müller, *A Narrative of Some of the Lord's Dealings with George Müller.*

[21] "Orphan Records," *Müllers*, The George Müller Charitable Trust, accessed May 16, 2015, http://www.mullers.org/orphanrecords.

[22] "The Bristol Miracle, An Account of God's Faithfulness to the Work of George Müller," *Müllers*, The George Müller Charitable Trust, accessed May 16, 2015, http://www.mullers.org/downloads/2014 TheBristolMiracle.pdf.

[23] "George Mueller, Orphanages Built by Prayer," *Christianity.com*, accessed May 16, 2015, http://www.christianity.com/church/church-history/church-history-for-kids/george-mueller-orphanages-built-by-prayer-11634869.html.

[24] Ed Reese, "James Hudson Taylor," *Worldwide Missions*, Wholesome Words, accessed May 18, 2015, http://www.wholesomewords.org/missions/biotaylor2.html.

[25] *Ibid.*

[26] *Ibid.*

[27] "Our Story Begins Video," *OMF Missions to East Asias People*, accessed May 17, 2015, http://omf.org/blog/2015/02/27/our-story-begins-video.

[28] Reese, "James Hudson Taylor."

[29] *Ibid.*

[30] *Ibid.*

[31] Clifford G. Howell, "J. Hudson Taylor: Founder of the China Inland Mission," *Worldwide Missions*, Wholesome Words, accessed May 18, 2015, http://www.wholesomewords.org/missions/biotaylor7.html.

[32] Reese, "James Hudson Taylor."

[33] Austin, *China's Millions*, 87–88.

[34] *Ibid.*, 167–168.

35 Marshall Broomhall, "Hudson Taylor: Chronology of Life," ed. Stephen Ross, *Worldwide Missions*, Wholesome Words, accessed May 19, 2015, http://www.wholesomewords.org/missions/biotaylor8.html.

36 Charles H. Cosgrove, Herold Weiss, and K. K. Yeo, *Cross-cultural Paul: Journeys to Others, Journeys to Ourselves* (Grand Rapids, MI: William. B. Eerdmans, 2005), 114.

37 *Ibid.*

38 John Pomfret, "'Autumn in the Heavenly Kingdom: China, the West, and the Epic Story of the Taiping Civil War' by Stephen R. Platt," *The Washington Post*, April 27, 2012, accessed May 19, 2015, https://www.washingtonpost.com/entertainment/books/autumn -in-the-heavenly-kingdom-china-the-west-and-the-epic-story-of-the-taiping-civil-war-by-stephen-r-platt/2012/04/27/gIQAQwJ3lT_story.html?utm_term=.953ac77aac 3e.

39 Larry Clinton Thompson, *William Scott Ament and the Boxer Rebellion Heroism, Hubris and the "ideal Missionary"* (Jefferson: McFarland, 2009), 14.

40 Kevin Xiyi Yao, "At the Turn of the Century: A Study of the China Centenary Missionary Conference of 1907," *International Bulletin of Missionary Research* 32.2 (2008): 65–70, accessed May 18, 2015, http://www.internationalbulletin.org/issues/2008-02/2008-02-065-yao.pdf.

41 *Ibid.*

42 Howard Culbertson, "A Chronology of Church History from the Perspective of the Expansion of Christianity," *Missions Time Line*, accessed May 18, 2015, http://home.snu.edu/~hculbert/line.htm.

43 "Our Story Begins Video."

44 Yao, "At the Turn of the Century."

[45] Henry Otis Dwight, H. Allen Tupper, and Edwin Munsell Bliss, *The Encyclopedia of Missions Descriptive, Historical, Biographical, Statistical*, 2d ed. (New York: Funk & Wagnalls, 1904), 824–825.

[46] Kenneth Scott Latourette, *A History of the Expansion of Christianity, Vol. IV, The Great Century A.D. 1800–A.D. 1914, Europe and the United States of America* (New York: Harper & Brothers, 1941).

[47] Albert Barnes, *Notes on the Bible* (Grand Rapids: Baker, 1885).

[48] *Ibid.*

[49] Gill, *John Gill's Exposition of the Entire Bible*.

CHAPTER 3

[1] "Mugwort (Artemisia vulgaris L.)," *Gernot Katzer's Spice Pages*, July 4, 2006, accessed April 20, 2015, http://www.gernot-katzers-spice-pages.com/engl/Arte_vul.html.

[2] "About Artemisia Vulgaris (Titepati in Nepali)," *Titepati's Blog*, June 19, 2009, accessed April 20, 2015, https://titepati.wordpress.com/about/.

[3] IAEA (International Atomic Energy Agency), "Ten years after Chernobyl: What do we really know? Based on the proceedings of the IAEA/WHO/EC international conference, Vienna, April 1996," *International Nuclear Information System* 28.20 (1997), accessed April 22, 2015, http://www.iaea.org/inis/collection/NCLCollectionStore/_Public/28/058/28058918.pdf.

[4] "20 years ago: Chernobyl," *Greenpeace International*, accessed June 23, 2013, http://www.greenpeace.org/international/en/multimedia/videos/Brilliant-Greenpeace-video-on-Chernobyl-/.

[5] *Ibid.*

[6] A.V. Yablokov, V.B. Nesterenko, and A.V. Nesterenko, "Chapter III. Consequences of the Chernobyl Catastrophe for the

Environment," *Annals of the New York Academy of Sciences*, 1181 (2009): 221–286, accessed June 19, 2016, http://onlinelibrary.wiley.com/doi/10.1111/j.1749-6632.2009.04830.x/full.

[7] "Chernobyl Disaster," *Wikipedia*, accessed May 28, 2013, http://en.wikipedia.org/wiki/Chernobyl_disaster.

[8] "Chernobyl, The Bitter Taste of Wormwood," dir. Haruki Kito, Hidemi Hyuga, and Takahiro Sekito, prod. Tetsuo Hirose, Kikuo Sasakawa, and Katzuhiko Hayashi, *Films for the Humanities*, 1993, Videocassette.

[9] *Ibid.*

[10] *Ibid.*

[11] *Ibid.*

[12] *Ibid.*

[13] *Ibid.*

[14] *Ibid.*

[15] *Ibid.*

[16] *Ibid.*

[17] *Ibid.*

[18] *Ibid.*

[19] *Ibid.*

[20] "Seconds from Disaster: Meltdown in Chernobyl," *National Geographic Channel*, 2004, online video.

[21] *Ibid.*

[22] Joseph H. Thayer, *Thayer's Greek English Lexicon of the New Testament* (Peabody, MA: Hendrickson, 1889).

[23] *Ibid.*

[24] Robert Jamieson, A. R. Fausset, and David Brown, *A Commentary on the Old and New Testaments* (1871).

[25] Thayer, *Thayer's Greek English Lexicon of the New Testament*.

[26] Marshall Beeber, "Scientific Scenario of a Comet's Impact and the 'Wormwood Star' Prophecy," *The Messianic Literary Corner*,

accessed May 28, 2013, http://www.messianic-literary.com/comet1.htm.

CHAPTER 4

[1] Matthew White, "Source List and Detailed Death Tolls for the Primary Megadeaths of the Twentieth Century," *Necrometrics*, accessed April 22, 2015, http://necrometrics.com/20c5m.htm.

[2] "Frequently Asked Questions," *Radiation Effects Research Foundation*, A Cooperative Japan-US Research Organization, accessed May 16, 2015, http://www.rerf.or.jp/general/qa_e/qa1.html.

[3] "U. S. Strategic Bombing Survey: The Effects of the Atomic Bombings of Hiroshima and Nagasaki, June 19, 1946. Truman Papers, President's Secretary's File. Atomic Bomb: Hiroshima and Nagasaki," *Harry S. Truman Presidential Library and Museum*, June 19, 1946, accessed April 1, 2016, https://www.trumanlibrary.org/whistlestop/study_collections/bomb/large/documents/index.php?documentid=65&pagenumber=11.

[4] "The 7 Trumpets DVD," prod. Irvin Baxter, *Endtime Ministries*, DVD.

[5] Joseph H. Thayer, *Thayer's Greek English Lexicon of the New Testament* (Peabody, MA: Hendrickson, 1889).

[6] John Malik, "The Yields of the Hiroshima and Nagasaki Explosions, Rep. no. LA-8819," *Los Alamos National Laboratory*, 1985, accessed May 16, 2015, http://atomicarchive.com/Docs/pdfs/00313791.pdf.

CHAPTER 5

[1] Matthew White, "Source List and Detailed Death Tolls for the Primary Megadeaths of the Twentieth Century," *Necrometrics*, accessed April 22, 2015, http://necrometrics.com/20c5m.htm.

2 Gary Sheffield, *War on the Western Front* (Oxford, U.K.: Osprey, 2007).

3 Stephen Bull and Adam Hook, *World War I Trench Warfare (2): 1916–18* (Oxford, U.K.: Osprey, 2002), 5.

4 Michael Duffy, "Weapons of War – Poison Gas," *FirstWorldWar.com*, accessed April 22, 2015, http://www.firstworldwar.com/weaponry/gas.htm.

5 Michael Duffy, "Weapons of War – Introduction," *FirstWorldWar.com*, accessed April 22, 2015, http://www.firstworldwar.com/weaponry/index.htm.

6 Michael Duffy, "Weapons of War – Trench Mortars," *FirstWorldWar.com*, accessed April 22, 2015, http://www.firstworldwar.com/weaponry/mortars.htm.

7 "World War I," accessed September 18, 2011, http://www.frontiernet.net/~mmulford/ww1.htm.

8 Marvin R. Vincent, *Vincent's Word Studies in the New Testament* (Hendrickson, 1888).

9 "The 7 Trumpets DVD," prod. Irvin Baxter, *Endtime Ministries*, DVD.

10 "Chernobyl, The Bitter Taste of Wormwood," dir. Haruki Kito, Hidemi Hyuga, and Takahiro Sekito, prod. Tetsuo Hirose, Kikuo Sasakawa, and Katzuhiko Hayashi, *Films for the Humanities*, 1993, Videocassette.

CHAPTER 6

1 "CHEMTRAILS Exposed on Discovery Channel," *YouTube*, accessed March 3, 2012, https://www.youtube.com/watch?v=yZFNJplylns.

2 *Ibid.*

3 "What is a contrail and how does it form?" *National Weather Service*, Western Region Headquarters, Salt Lake City, NOAA, http://www.wrh.noaa.gov/fgz/science/contrail.php.

[4] Mick West, "Contrail Grids are not Chemtrail Grids," *Contrail Science,* accessed March 3, 2016, http://contrailscience.com/contrail-grids-are-not-chemtrail-grids/.

[5] "CHEMTRAILS Exposed on Discovery Channel."

[6] "H. R. 2977, 107TH CONGRESS 1ST SESSION," *U.S. Government Publishing Office,* accessed May 28, 2013, http://www.gpo.gov/fdsys/pkg/BILLS-107hr2977ih/pdf/BILLS-107hr2977ih.pdf.

[7] *Ibid.*

[8] "Bill Summary & Status, 107th Congress (2001–2002), H.R.2977," *The Library of Congress,* USA.gov, accessed May 28, 2013, https://www.congress.gov/bill/107th-congress/house-bill/2977.

[9] "H.R.3657 – Space Preservation Act of 2003, 108th Congress (2003–2004)," *The Library of Congress,* USA.gov, accessed May 28, 2013, https://www.congress.gov/bill/108th-congress/house-bill/3657/text.

[10] "H.R.2420 – Space Preservation Act of 2005, 109th Congress (2005–2006)," *The Library of Congress,* USA.gov, accessed May 28, 2013, https://www.congress.gov/bill/109th-congress/house-bill/2420/text.

[11] "Report to the Honorable Harry Reid, U.S. Senate, 'Environmental Protection: DOD Management Issues Related to Chaff,'" Rep. no. B-279055, *U.S. General Accounting Office,* 1998, accessed April 23, 2015, http://gao.gov/products/NSIAD-98-219.

[12] *Ibid.*

[13] *Ibid.*

[14] "Chemtrails: GAO Report Admits 'chaff,'" *The Idaho Observer,* July 2006, accessed May 28, 2013, http://www.proliberty.com/observer/20060704.htm.

[15] "Environmental Protection: DOD Management Issues Related to Chaff."

[16] Beate G. Liepert, "Recent Changes in Solar Radiation under Cloudy Conditions in Germany," *International Journal of Climatology,* 17.14 (1997): 1581–1593, http://onlinelibrary.wiley.com/doi/10.1002/(SICI)1097-0088(19971130)17:14%3C1581::AID-JOC214%3E3.0.CO;2-H/pdf.

[17] *Ibid.*

[18] David J. Travis, Andrew M. Carleton, and Ryan G. Lauritsen, "Climatology: Contrails reduce daily temperature range," *Nature,* 418, 601 (August 8, 2002), doi:10.1038/418601a.

[19] Beate G. Liepert, and George J. Kukla, "Decline in Global Solar Radiation with Increased Horizontal Visibility in Germany between 1964 and 1990," *J. Climate* 10.9 (1997): 2391–401, http://journals.ametsoc.org/doi/pdf/10.1175/1520-0442%281997%29010%3C2391%3ADIGSRW%3E2.0.CO%3B2.

[20] Xiaobo Zheng, Weimin Kang, Tianliang Zhao, Yuxiang Luo, Changchun Duan, and Juan Chen, "Long-term Trends in Sunshine Duration over Yunnan-Guizhou Plateau in Southwest China for 1961–2005," *Geophys. Res. Lett.,* 35.15 (2008): 1961–2005, http://onlinelibrary.wiley.com/doi/10.1029/2008GL034482/full.

[21] *Ibid.*

[22] *Ibid.*

[23] Tomoshige Inoue and Jun Matsumoto, "Seasonal and Secular Variations of Sunshine Duration and Natural Seasons in Japan," *International Journal of Climatology,* 23 (2003): 1219–1234, http://onlinelibrary.wiley.com/doi/10.1002/joc.933/epdf.

[24] Beate G. Liepert, "Global Dimming," *Lamont-Doherty Earth Observatory,* Columbia University, accessed June 17, 2016, http://www.ldeo.columbia.edu/research/biology-paleo-environment/global-dimming.

[25] Beate G. Liepert, "Observed reductions of surface solar radiation at sites in the United States and worldwide from 1961 to 1990," *Geophysical Research Letters,* Vol. 29, No.10, 1421 (2002),

doi:10.1029/2002GL014910,
http://onlinelibrary.wiley.com/doi/10.1029/2002GL014910/full.

[26] Liepert, "Global Dimming."

[27] "Global Dimming Programme transcript," *BBC*, September 17, 2014, accessed June 17, 2016, http://www.bbc.co.uk/sn/tvradio/programmes/horizon/dimming _trans.shtml.

[28] Liepert, "Global Dimming."

[29] *Ibid.*

[30] Zheng et al., "Long-term Trends in Sunshine Duration over Yunnan-Guizhou Plateau in Southwest China for 1961–2005."

[31] "Global Dimming Programme transcript."

[32] *Ibid.*

[33] Jeffrey Pollack, "Oil Spill: After the Deluge," *Duke Magazine*, Volume 89, No.3, March-April 2003, accessed November 14, 2016, https://web.archive.org/web/20100613021006/http://www.dukem agazine.duke.edu/dukemag/issues/030403/oil1.html.

[34] Bernard Rostker, "Environmental Exposure Report, Oil Well Fires, III. CHRONOLOGY OF EVENTS," *Department of Defense*, accessed November 14, 2016, http://www.gulflink.osd.mil/owf_ii/owf_ii_s03.htm#III.%20CHR ONOLOGY%20OF%20EVENTS.

CHAPTER 7

[1] Explainer, "What's the Name of Saddam Hussein?" *The Slate Group*, November 16, 1998, accessed June 23, 2015, http://www.slate.com/articles/news_and_politics/explainer/1998/ 11/whats_the_name_of_saddam_hussein.html.

[2] Ervin Baxter, "Saddam Hussein in the Bible," *Endtime Ministries*, November 6, 2002, accessed February 23, 2012, http://www.endtime.com/endtime-magazine-articles/saddam-hussein-in-the-bible/.

[3] John Gill, *John Gill's Exposition of the Entire Bible* (1746-1766).

[4] Carl Conetta, "The Wages of War," *The Project on Defense Alternatives (PDA)*, The Commonwealth Institute, October 20, 2003, accessed November 22, 2016, http://www.comw.org/pda/0310rm8ap2.html#1.%20Iraqi%20civi lian%20fatalities%20in%20the%201991%20Gulf.

[5] Seymour M. Hersh, "Torture at Abu Ghraib - The New Yorker," *Annals of National Security, The New Yorker*, May 10, 2004, accessed April 20, 2015, http://www.newyorker.com/magazine/2004/05/10/torture-at-abu-ghraib.

[6] Americaisbabylon, "(9) 5th Trumpet Prophecy Fulfilled - Operation Iraqi Freedom," *YouTube*, October 4, 2012, accessed May 5, 2013, https://www.youtube.com/watch?v=hAfXwvobdNc.

[7] Martha Raddatz, "Tape Shows Apache Pilots Firing on Iraqis," *ABC News*, January 9, 2004, accessed April 20, 2015, http://abcnews.go.com/WNT/story?id=131481&page=1.

[8] "Iraq: Human Rights Must Be Foundation for Rebuilding," Rep. No. 148, *London: Amnesty International*, June 20, 2003, accessed April 20, 2015, https://www.amnesty.org/download/Documents/108000/mde141 362003en.pdf.

[9] Hersh, "Torture at Abu Ghraib - The New Yorker."

[10] Americaisbabylon, "(9) 5th Trumpet Prophecy Fulfilled - Operation Iraqi Freedom."

[11] Charles J. Hanley, "In Iraq -- AP Enterprise: Former Iraqi Detainees Tell of Riots, Punishment in the Sun, Good Americans and Pitiless Ones," *U-T San Diego, San Diego Union Tribune*, November 1, 2003, accessed April 20, 2015, http://legacy.utsandiego.com/news/world/iraq/20031101-0936-iraq-thecamps.html.

[12] Seth Hettena, "Reports Detail Abu Ghraib Prison Death; Was It Torture?" *NBCNews.com*, February 17, 2005, accessed April 20, 2015, http://www.nbcnews.com/id/6988054/.

[13] Patrick Baz, "22 Killed in Baghdad Mortar Attack," *USATODAY.com*, April 20, 2004, accessed April 20, 2015, http://usatoday30.usatoday.com/news/world/iraq/2004-04-20-iraq_x.htm.

[14] "The Road to Abu Ghraib," *Human Rights Watch*, June 9, 2004, accessed June 25, 2015, http://www.hrw.org/reports/2004/06/08/road-abu-ghraib.

[15] "Inmates Transferred out of Abu Ghraib as Coalition Hands off Control," *Boston.com*, September 3, 2006, accessed April 20, 2015, http://www.boston.com/news/world/middleeast/articles/2006/09/03/inmates_transferred_out_of_abu_ghraib_as_coalition_hands_off_control/.

[16] Ernest Scheyder, "BP Estimates Oil Spill up to 100,000 Barrels per Day in Document," *Reuters*, June 20, 2010, accessed April 25, 2015, http://www.reuters.com/article/2010/06/20/us-oil-spill-idUSN1416392020100620.

[17] Joseph Chiappalone, "Gassed In The Gulf - Benzene, New Gulf War Syndrome," *Rense.com*, by Deborah Dupré, June 22, 2010, accessed April 25, 2015, http://www.rense.com/general91/spin.htm.

[18] Tim McDonnell, "VIDEO: Is the BP Oil Spill Cleanup Still Making People Sick?" *Mother Jones and the Foundation for National Progress*, May 16, 2014, accessed June 17, 2016, http://www.motherjones.com/blue-marble/2014/05/bp-oil-spill-cleanup-still-making-people-sick.

[19] James Strong, *Strong's Hebrew and Greek Dictionaries* (1890).

[20] Joseph H. Thayer, *Thayer's Greek English Lexicon of the New Testament* (Peabody, MA: Hendrickson, 1889).

[21] *Ibid.*

[22] "Macondo Prospect, Gulf of Mexico, United States of America," *Offshore-technology.com*, accessed April 9, 2015, http://www.offshore-technology.com/projects/macondoprospect/.

[23] The CNN Wire Staff, "Oil Slick Spreads from Sunken Rig," *CNN*, April 22, 2010, accessed April 22, 2015, http://edition.cnn.com/2010/US/04/22/oil.rig.explosion/index.html.

[24] Ponisseril Somasundaran, Partha Patra, Raymond S. Farinato, and Kyriakos Papadopoulos, eds., *Oil Spill Remediation: Colloid Chemistry-Based Principles and Solutions*, First Edition (John Wiley & Sons, Inc., 2014), 65, accessed November 5, 2016, http://ourenvironment.berkeley.edu/wp-content/uploads/2011/07/Ch3.pdf.

[25] Jonathan L. Ramseur, "Deepwater Horizon oil spill: The Fate of the Oil," *Congressional Research Service*, 7–5700, R41531 (2010): 8, accessed November 5, 2016, https://www.fas.org/sgp/crs/misc/R41531.pdf.

[26] Mark Huber, "The Other Gulf War," *Air & Space Magazine*, Smithsonian, January 2011, accessed April 22, 2015, http://www.airspacemag.com/flight-today/the-other-gulf-war-66923095/?no-ist=.

[27] *Ibid.*

[28] Alun Lewis, "Oil Spill Dispersant Use at the Deepwater Horizon Incident," *Offshore Arabia Conference & Exhibition* (2014).

[29] Huber, "The Other Gulf War."

[30] *Ibid.*

[31] Lewis, "Oil Spill Dispersant Use at the Deepwater Horizon Incident."

[32] *Ibid.*

[33] Huber, "The Other Gulf War."

[34] "On Scene Coordinator Report: Deepwater Horizon Oil Spill," *Washington, D.C.: U.S. Dept. of Homeland Security, U.S. Coast Guard,* September 2011, accessed May 18, 2013, http://www.uscg.mil/foia/docs/dwh/fosc_dwh_report.pdf.

[35] "HC-130H: Hercules," *Office of Aviation Forces (CG-711), U.S. Coast Guard,* accessed April 22, 2015, http://www.uscg.mil/hq/cg7/cg711/c130h.asp.

[36] Thayer, *Thayer's Greek English Lexicon of the New Testament.*

[37] Photo by Auréola, https://commons.wikimedia.org/wiki/File:Latin_Poet_Ovid.jpg.

[38] Credit: © AbZahri AbAzizis, CC BY 2.0, http://commons.wikimedia.org/wiki/File:Panthera_leo_-zoo_-yawning-8a.jpg, size changed.

[39] Huber, "The Other Gulf War."

[40] Credit: © Didier Descouens, CC BY-SA 3.0, http://commons.wikimedia.org/wiki/File:Titanacris_Albipes_Vol.jpg, size changed.

[41] Thayer, *Thayer's Greek English Lexicon of the New Testament.*

[42] David Kirby, "Corexit, Oil Dispersant Used By BP, Is Destroying Gulf Marine Life, Scientists Say," *The Huffington Post,* April 25, 2013, accessed April 22, 2015, http://www.huffingtonpost.com/2013/04/25/corexit-bp-oil-dispersant_n_3157080.html.

[43] Mark Hertsgaard, "What BP Doesn't Want You to Know About the 2010 Gulf Spill," *Newsweek,* April 22, 2013, accessed April 22, 2015, http://www.newsweek.com/what-bp-doesnt-want-you-know-about-2010-gulf-spill-63015.

[44] *Ibid.*

[45] *Ibid.*

[46] "Tears: Sickened Cleanup Worker Praying That God Will Just Let Him Die (VIDEO)," *Florida Oil Spill Law RSS,* April 1, 2011, accessed April 20, 2015, http://www.floridaoilspilllaw.com/tears-

sickened-cleanup-worker-praying-that-god-will-just-let-him-die-video/.

[47] Sir Robert Anderson, *The Coming Prince* (London: Hodder & Stoughton, 1894).

[48] "Deepwater Horizon Containment and Response: Harnessing Capabilities and Lessons Learned," *BP-report* (September 1, 2010): 55, accessed May 18, 2013, http://media.washingtonpost.com/wp-srv/gulf-coast-oil-spill/bp-report.pdf.

[49] "On Scene Coordinator Report: Deepwater Horizon Oil Spill."

[50] Thayer, *Thayer's Greek English Lexicon of the New Testament.*

[51] Lewis, "Oil Spill Dispersant Use at the Deepwater Horizon Incident."

[52] "On Scene Coordinator Report: Deepwater Horizon Oil Spill."

[53] *Ibid.*

[54] Harry R. Weber, "Blown-out BP Well Finally Killed at Bottom of Gulf," *Boston.com*, September 19, 2010, accessed May 18, 2013, http://www.boston.com/news/nation/articles/2010/09/19/blown_out_bp_well_finally_killed_at_bottom_of_gulf/.

[55] *Ibid.*

[56] H.W.F. Gesenius, *Gesenius' Hebrew and Chaldee Lexicon to the Old Testament Scriptures* (London: Samuel Bagster & Sons, 1857).

[57] Strong, *Strong's Hebrew and Greek Dictionaries.*

[58] A. T. Robertson, *Word Pictures in the New Testament* (Nashville, Tenn.: Broadman, 1930).

[59] Jim Garamone, "'CINC' Is Sunk," *DoD News*, American Forces Press Service, October 25, 2002, accessed November 15, 2016, http://archive.defense.gov/news/newsarticle.aspx?id=42568.

[60] "Newsweek Depiction of Obama as Lord Shiva Upsets Some Indian-Americans," *FoxNews.com*, November 21, 2010, accessed November 15, 2016,

http://www.foxnews.com/politics/2010/11/21/newsweek-depiction-obama-lord-shiva-upsets-indians.html.

[61] David Limbaugh, *The Great Destroyer: Barack Obama's War on the Republic* (Regnery Publishing, 2012), Inside flap.

[62] Brian Tashman, "Renew America Pundit Says 'Obama, From Birth, Was The Chosen Destroyer Of America,'" *Right Wing Watch*, June 12, 2014, accessed November 15, 2016, http://www.rightwingwatch.org/post/renew-america-pundit-says-obama-from-birth-was-the-chosen-destroyer-of-america/.

[63] Andrew Solomon, "Obamacare the Destroyer: How It Has Hurt Small Business," *American Thinker*, November 15, 2016, accessed November 15, 2016, http://www.americanthinker.com/articles/2016/11/obamacare_the_destroyer_how_it_has_hurt_small_business.html.

[64] Robertson, *Word Pictures in the New Testament*.

CHAPTER 8

[1] Joseph H. Thayer, *Thayer's Greek English Lexicon of the New Testament* (Peabody, MA: Hendrickson, 1889).

[2] "Pregnancy Symptom: Contractions," *Pregnancy Information Center*, *MedHelp*, accessed May 20, 2013, http://www.medhelp.org/tags/health_page/28/Pregnancy/Pregnancy-Symptom-Contractions?hp_id=1055.

[3] Thomas Carson and Mary Bonk, "World War II," in *Gale Encyclopedia of U.S. Economic History* (Detroit: Gale Group, 1999), accessed May 26, 2015, http://ic.galegroup.com/ic/suic/ReferenceDetailsPage/ReferenceDetailsWindow?displayGroupName=K12-Reference&action=2&catId=GALE%7C00000000MJ0W&documentId=GALE%7CEJ1667500771&userGroupName=sain62671&jsid=e67b11dca13ba2d569cf1d8cef98d826.

4 Matthew White, "Second World War (1939-45): 66,000,000," *Necrometrics*, accessed April 22, 2015, http://necrometrics.com/20c5m.htm#Second.

5 "World Population," *International Programs*, U.S. Census Bureau, accessed November 16, 2016, http://www.census.gov/population/international/data/worldpop /table_history.php.

6 Robert Jamieson, A. R. Fausset, and David Brown, *A Commentary on the Old and New Testaments* (1871).

7 Thayer, *Thayer's Greek English Lexicon of the New Testament*.

8 A. T. Robertson, *Word Pictures in the New Testament* (Nashville, Tenn.: Broadman, 1930).

9 "SA-8 GECKO 9K33M3 Osa-AKM," *Military Analysis Network*, accessed June 13, 2016, http://fas.org/man/dod-101/sys/missile/row/sa-8.htm.

10 Credit: © Ştefan Ciocan, CC BY-SA 3.0, https://commons.wikimedia.org/wiki/File:Romanian_SA-8.jpg, size changed.

11 "Video: Russia test-launches missiles during planned military drills," *RT*, May 8, 2014, accessed December 5, 2016, https://www.youtube.com/watch?v=v71eF8HdZb8.

12 Albert Barnes, *Notes on the Bible* (Grand Rapids: Baker, 1885).

13 Marvin R. Vincent, *Vincent's Word Studies in the New Testament* (Hendrickson, 1888).

14 Diaa Hadid, "Syrian Rebels And Government Reach Truce In Besieged Area," *The Huffington Post*, January 15, 2015, accessed April 22, 2015, http://www.huffingtonpost.com/2015/01/15/syria-rebel-truce_n_6478226.html.

15 Vincent, *Vincent's Word Studies in the New Testament*.

16 Barnes, *Notes on the Bible*.

17 Jamieson et al., *A Commentary on the Old and New Testaments*.

18 John Gill, *John Gill's Exposition of the Entire Bible* (1746-1766).

[19] *Ibid.*

[20] "Official Reports: Decision Adopted by the Executive Committee, Bulletin Du Comité International Olympique," *Olympic Review* 25.32 (1951), accessed April 22, 2015, http://library.la84.org/OlympicInformationCenter/OlympicRevie w/1951/BDCE25/BDCE25s.pdf.

[21] The idea of applying the Olympics' color designation on continents to the color of the breastplates was first suggested by Dr. C. Song.

CHAPTER 9

[1] James Strong, *Strong's Hebrew and Greek Dictionaries* (1890).

[2] John Gill, *John Gill's Exposition of the Entire Bible* (1746-1766).

[3] Albert Barnes, *Notes on the Bible* (Grand Rapids: Baker, 1885).

[4] Adam Clarke, *Adam Clarke's Commentary on the Bible* (New York: Abingdon, 1829).

[5] Marvin R. Vincent, *Vincent's Word Studies in the New Testament* (Peabody, MA: Hendrickson, 1888).

[6] *The Chokmah Commentary* (Christian Wisdom Company, 1993).

[7] Strong, *Strong's Hebrew and Greek Dictionaries.*

[8] Clarke, *Adam Clarke's Commentary on the Bible.*

[9] Barnes, *Notes on the Bible.*

[10] Joseph H. Thayer, *Thayer's Greek English Lexicon of the New Testament* (Peabody, MA: Hendrickson, 1889).

[11] Gill, *John Gill's Exposition of the Entire Bible.*

[12] Barnes, *Notes on the Bible.*

[13] Thayer, *Thayer's Greek English Lexicon of the New Testament.*

CHAPTER 10

[1] Surendre M. Verma, *The Mystery of the Tunguska Fireball* (Cambridge: Totem, 2006), 44.

2 Dan Good, "Planet X or Nibiru is headed for Earth, doomsayers believe," *New York Daily News*, January 21, 2016, accessed November 8, 2016, http://www.nydailynews.com/news/national/planet-x-nibiru-headed-earth-doomsayers-article-1.2504846.

3 Paul Chodas, Jon Giorgini, and Don Yeomans, "Near-Earth Asteroid 2012 DA14 to Miss Earth on February 15, 2013," *NASA/JPL Near-Earth Object Program Office*, March 6, 2012, accessed June 13, 2016, http://neo.jpl.nasa.gov/news/news174.html.

4 "Blast It or Paint It: Asteroid to Threaten Earth in 2013," *Russia Today*, March 3, 2012, accessed March 4, 2012, http://rt.com/news/paint-asteroid-earth-nasa-767/.

5 Dave Hunt, *A Woman Rides the Beast: The Roman Catholic Church and the Last Days* (Harvest House, 1994).

6 Joseph H. Thayer, *Thayer's Greek English Lexicon of the New Testament* (Peabody, MA: Hendrickson, 1889).

Made in the USA
Columbia, SC
20 November 2020